THE PRIVATE EYE ANNUAL 2001

EDITED BY IAN HISLOP

PRODUCT RECALL

BRITAIN

(No. 74732461)

The manufacturers regret that a number of serious problems have recently emerged with this product.

Millions of complaints have been received regarding the constituent parts of Britain – none of which appear to work. Furthermore, some of them are extremely dangerous and can cause serious injury.

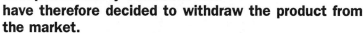

The manufacturers regret that Britain no longer conforms to acceptable safety standards and have therefore decided to withdraw the product from the market.

Issued by UK PLC – "Disasters R Us"

Published in Great Britain by
Private Eye Productions Ltd
6 Carlisle Street, London W1D 5BN

© 2001 Pressdram Ltd
ISBN 1 901784 223
Designed by Bridget Tisdall
Printed in England by
Ebenezer Baylis & Son Ltd, Worcester

2 4 6 8 10 9 7 5 3

THE PRIVATE EYE ANNUAL 2001

EDITED BY IAN HISLOP

"I love it! Can you dumb it down for TV?"

CENSUS 2001

EVERY 10 YEARS Private Eye conducts a census of its readers, in order to enable our marketing department to develop forward-planning initiatives and editorial policy.

This census form *must* be filled in by all readers, at exactly the same time — ie, between 2 and 4am on the morning of Sunday 6 May, 2001.

Failure to complete all 397 sections of the form is a criminal offence, punishable by a fine not exceeding £5,000 or death.

IDENTIFICATION

1 Please give full names and address, including postal code, of all persons in the household at 2am on 6 May, including visiting relatives, non-live-in partners staying one night only, burglars visiting the property for professional reasons and domestic pets (excluding fish).

RELATIONSHIPS

2 Explain the exact relationship between each member of your household. If Person A (the main householder) is the live-in partner of Person B, but not the father or mother of Persons C, D, E or F, then he or she should ignore this question and go straight to Question 9B.

RACE

3 **Which of the following descriptions corresponds most closely to your ethnic origin?**
a) White (no sugar) ☐
b) White (with two sugars) ☐
c) Afro-Welsh-Oriental ☐
d) Irish-Asian ☐
e) German Shepherd ☐
f) Chicken Tikka Masala ☐
g) Robin Cook ☐

RELIGION *(optional)*

4 **Do you practise any of the following world religions?**
a) Church of Scientology ☐
b) Acupuncture ☐
c) Aromatherapy ☐
d) Jews For Islam ☐
e) Opus Dei ☐
f) Chicken Tikka Masala ☐

WORKING TIME

5 **How many hours a week do you work at your principal place of employment?**
a) 10-15 ☐
b) More than 65 ☐
c) Self-employed ☐
d) Retired over 75 ☐

Those on benefit should skip this question and report to the Job Centre within one week, or else face penalties up to £5,000.

HOUSEHOLD FACILITIES

6 **How many toilets are there in your house?**
a) Up to 10 ☐
b) More than 20 ☐
c) None ☐

If c), skip question, and go out of window.

How many times, on average, do you and members of your household use the toilet per month?
a) Over 170 ☐
b) Between 123 and 169 ☐
c) Ask the audience ☐
d) None ☐

If d), consult a General Practitioner immediately.

LIFESTYLE

7 **What is the number owned by your household of:**
a) Lawnmowers ☐
b) Pyjamas (males only) ☐
c) Grapefruit segments ☐
d) Zimmer frames ☐
e) Unsolicited free copies of The Spectator ☐

POLITICS

8 **Who is your favourite television personality?**
a) ITN's Trevor McDonald ☐
b) Call Nick Ross ☐
c) Ulrika Jonsson ☐
d) Anne Robinson ☐
e) TV's Charles Moore ☐

SEXUALITY

9 **In which of the following locations do you normally engage in sexual congress?**
a) Bedroom ☐
b) Living room settee ☐
c) Desk in office ☐
d) Broom cupboard in restaurant ☐
e) NCP Car Park ☐
f) Chicken Tikka Masala ☐

The Daily Lorrygraph
(incorporating the Daily Male Motorist) — Friday, 22 September 2000

Heroic Strikers Hold Country to Ransom

BY OUR ENTIRE STAFF
CHARLES MOORESTRIKESPLEASE

BRITAIN was yesterday brought to its knees by courageous bands of picketing farmers, hauliers and taxi drivers.

Shouting "Smash the system!" and "Bring down the government!", these honest sons-of-toil won the backing of the entire country in their desire to pay less money for their petrol.

Hang Blair

IT IS a cause which has struck a thrilling chord in the hearts of every man, woman and child in Britain, millions of whom were yesterday cheering on the efforts of the ringleaders to reduce the entire nation to a state of complete chaos and misery.

The Daily Mailograph Says

MAKE no mistake. This is democracy in action. When the people speak, the government must listen. All of Britain's precious freedoms were won on the picket line, by brave men and women who believed in free petrol *(Surely "freedom"? Ed.)*. You only have to remember the Suffragettes, the Tolpuddle Martyrs, the Poll Tax, the Peasants' Revolt, to see what can be done when the British people are finally stirred to action.

To the brave pickets, the Mailograph says "Britain salutes you".

Letters to the Editor

SIR – Am I the only one whose heart has rejoiced at the sight of miles of empty road, entirely free of cars. When I was driving along looking for a petrol station yesterday, the roads were gloriously free of gas-guzzling juggernauts and selfish women on school runs. And aren't the supermarkets wonderfully empty of food *(Surely "fellow-shoppers")*?
REGINALD GIMSON
Dimwittering, Sussex

SIR – Mr Blair and his cohorts will not defeat the British people, any more than did his forerunner Herr Hitler in the dark days of the Winter of Discontent. This morning when my neighbour stopped to offer me a lift to work, I was reminded of the spirit of the Blitz. On the train, instead of everyone reading the newspapers, we all took out our lap tops and wrote letters to you instead.
CARRIAGE B, the 7.14, Connex South East, Robertsbridge to Charing Cross (just passing the London Eye)

SIR – What is all this fuss about people getting to work? I had no problem at all yesterday since I am retired.
DAVID CASHEW-NUTT
Poujade-sur-Mer, France

SIR – Your readers may be interested to know how I got to my office yesterday. I began my journey at 4.32am on a pair of roller-blades borrowed from my daughter Emma. The second stage involved a micro-light aircraft flown by my neighbour, Wing Commander Dan Duxford DSC and Bar. This mode of transport was sufficient for me to arrive at Wallingford Station, in time to catch a motor cruiser which took me all the way down the Thames to Greenwich, from where the Docklands Light Railway delivered me to my desk at 5.32pm just in time to go home again.
MAURICE STREPSIL
The Old Pharmacy, Byfleet

SIR – Has Mr Blair considered turning his precious Dome into a service station?
MIKE GIGGLER
Via e-mail

Irresponsible Hooligans Hold Country To Ransom

by Our Entire Staff
Polly Putthestrikersingaol

Britain was yesterday brought to its knees by a tiny clique of National Front-supporting Poujadiste owners of lorry firms and racist taxi drivers.

This criminal fringe is determined to overthrow the lawfully-elected Government of Mr Blair in defiance of the vast majority of law-abiding folk.

We Love Tony

There is no popular support whatever for these thugs and murderers in their wholesale assault on all civilised values.

It is high time that the police and SAS were sent in to smash these so-called secondary picketers once and for all.

The Cardian Says

We salute Mrs Thatcher in her crucial hour of need. It is time for the smack of firm government. Do they not realise that thousands of toddlers are starving in our hospitals, and millions of OAPs are dying of hypothermia in this Indian Summer of Discontent? We say hats off to Herr Mussolini who at least kept the trains running on time.

Letters

The selfish motorists who are whingeing about a few pence on the price of petrol are completely missing the point. Only when we have petrol costing thousands of pounds a litre will the future of the planet be assured. Mr Blair must stand firm and support the ozone layer.
Crispin de Greene
Tickell College, Oxford

Once again, totally predictably, the Tory media have scapegoated the government rather than the real villain of the piece, ie the multi-national companies working to their hidden agenda of globalism who are deliberately restricting the supply of oil in order to make more money by not selling it.
D. Spart
Editor, Living Globalism, Hackney

I am a nurse, my partner is a social worker and my brother is a teacher.
Sue Flutt,
Salford

There is one blindingly obvious solution to the so-called fuel crisis. It involves using your legs. Walk, you lazy lot.
Dr Ranjit Rusbridger,
Edinburgh

Has it occurred to Tony Blair to use his Dome as a lorry park?
Mike Giggler
Via e-mail

PANIC AS FUEL STORIES DRY UP

by Our Energy Staff
Petrolella Wyatt

THERE were scenes of mass hysteria in Britain's newsrooms as the supply of stories of fuel shortages began to peter out.

The first signs were in Canary Wharf where desperate journalists were seen fighting over a story about a man in a Volvo losing his temper in a petrol station queue near Guildford. Said one gloomy editor, "By the end of the week there will be no petrol stories at all. The papers will be empty. Fleet Street will grind to a halt."

But a newspaper expert, Roy Greenparty, said "The papers have only themselves to blame. They have all been rushing to fill up their news pages with petrol stories with no thought for the future."

Bottom of Barell

He continued: "Now ordinary papers like the Telegraph will have to find alternative means to get through the week. And let's be honest, the occasional delivery of a picture of Liz Hurley without any clothes on is not going to satisfy anyone."

ON OTHER PAGES

Army to be sent into
Daily Mail **2-94**

Do we really want the country to be run by a small self-interested group who are only concerned with protecting their own jobs, like...er...?

A Taxi Driver writes

Every week a well-known cab driver is invited to comment on an issue of topical importance. THIS WEEK: The Fuel Crisis by **Ken Snotter**, Cab No. 613926

See those cabbies bringing London to a halt and holding the country to ransom? Brilliant, eh? Know what I'd do to those cabbies? Give 'em all a knighthood. That's the only sort of language they understand. Fantastic! You don't know anywhere round your way where I could get any diesel, do you guv? We just ran out. You'll have to walk the rest. I 'ad that Andrew Marr in the back once. 'e looks different on the telly.

NEXT WEEK: Paul Dacre (Cab No. 9386124) on what we have to learn from the French.

THE FRENCH
An Apology

IN COMMON with all other newspapers we recently made a number of unwarranted attacks on the French strikers, government and general public.

● We suggested that the French lorry drivers were irresponsible, self-seeking anarchists and were acting in a fashion which had long been abandoned in modern Britain.

● We suggested the French Government was weak and spineless for subsequently giving in to their demand for fuel tax to be cut.

● We suggested the French populace were sentimental and typically Gallic in their deluded romantic attachment to mob rule.

We now realise that the above were entirely untrue and accept that:

● Like their heroic confrères across the channel, the British protestors have struck a proud blow for freedom and democracy.

● The British Government are spineless and feeble and should immediately give in to the protestors to lower the price of fuel.

● The British people have shown their true mettle in standing up to a repressive government and stockpiling as much milk as they could. *(Surely "making their voices heard"?)*

We apologise for any confusion caused to our readers by our earlier article.

POLICE 'TOOK NO ACTION' DURING PETROL CARNIVAL

by Our Home Affairs Staff
Phil Tank

THE police were accused of standing idly by during last week's Stopping Oil Festival, while revellers openly flouted the law and many acts of violence occurred.

But the organisers of the festival, who wished to remain nameless, said "everyone had a great time. The sun shone, the party-goers sang and danced and talked to Radio 4 reporters, and the police fully entered into the spirit of the occasion."

Last night the Home Office admitted that the police had turned a blind eye to many breaches of law and order, and said the Government was considering banning any future repetition of the carnival.

Unleaded Bliss

"The only alternative," said a spokesman, "is to move the festival back to France where it came from. It is not part of our tradition or culture and it ties up the police when they could be doing something more useful like giving each other anti-racism lectures."

I Love The Seventies
BBC2 (Sat 9.00pm)

Britain's truckers and farmers present a nostalgic tribute to those crazy days of Summer 1979 as industrial action humiliates a Labour Government, bringing Britain to a near standstill.

ADAM AND EVE VOTED OUT

by Our Paradise Staff
Jenny Siss

IN A shock climax to the sociological experiment that the whole of creation has been watching, the likeable Adam and the flirty Eve were sensationally cast out by a panel of viewers (God).

Adam and Eve had been living in the Garden for months and had been set a number of simple tasks – naming the animals, delving and spinning and not eating the apple.

Eve's Dropping

But they failed at the last challenge and ate the apple egged on by the Machiavellian "Nasty Old Nick".

The viewer (God) saw Nick pretending to be a serpent (against the rules) and persuading Eve to have a bite.

She and Adam then became involved in steamy scenes, including a sensual massage, snogging and uninhibited "begetting" under the tree of knowledge.

Channel Fall

But the audience (God) had had enough of their antics and voted them both out of Eden.

Said a disappointed God, "They're all ghastly and selfish. All they think about is sex. They have failed utterly."

Said Eve last night, "Obviously,

I'm gutted. I was never given a chance. I blame Nasty Old Nick for ruining my chance of winning the top prize of eternal life."

The couple have now sold their stories for an undisclosed sum to the Old Testament.

MILLENNIUM DAME TO BE SCRAPPED

by Our Political Staff
Andrew Marrvellous

THE symbol of New Labour is to be pulled down after the Government conceded that "it has no viable future".

The Millennium Dame was designed to be the most popular attraction in the whole of Britain, and was enthusiastically supported by the Government.

Mowlemmium Experience

The Dame, as it became known, was acclaimed by the Prime Minister as new, modern, exciting, touchy-feely and "guaranteed to produce the Wow Factor".

Tony Blair even promised that the Dame would last for twenty-five years.

But the popularity failed to materialise and a whispering campaign in the media branded the Dame "a flop".

Word of mouth spread and soon people were openly critical of the so-called "One Amazing Mo".

"It is all presentation," said one critic (a Mr P. Mandelson from Hartlepool). "There is no content at all. It's boring, lacking in ideas and it doesn't work."

Disaster Zone

He continued, "The Dame was in the wrong place at the wrong time – ie, in my way. Let's scrap it now and get it over with."

The Dame is to be bought by businessman Rupert Murdoch who plans to turn her into a book.

The Eye Names And Shames
THE DOMOPHILES

Here at last, as a public service, the Eye is proud to identify the guilty men who have been responsible for bringing disgrace on Britain.

 Simon Jenkins, 65. Behind his respectable pose as a former Editor of the Times, Jenkins is probably Britain's most dangerous Domophile.

 Charles "Charlie" Falconer, 71. Behind his respectable pose as a close friend of Tony Blair's, Falconer is a proven lawyer and has practised Domophilia for several years.

 Peter "Mandy" Mandelson, 41. Behind his respectable pose as the country's most powerful homosexual, Mandelson was long the organiser of the country's chief Domophile ring, including Alan Botney, Michael Grade, Lord Rogers and the prime minister himself.

GEORGE W. BUSH – NEW SHOCK

I'm not dyslexic — I've never even been to Dyslexia

HUNTER

THE PAEDOPHILE AND VIGILANTES

PORTSMOUTH RD.

OLYMPIC DRUG SHOCK

by Our Olympics Correspondent **Anna Bolic-Steroid**

THE entire Olympic movement reacted with shock and dismay today after a leading athlete arriving in Sydney was found not to be taking drugs.

"I stupidly thought I could win by sticking to the rules," said the disgraced star. "I now accept that training hard and eating sensibly was not the way to win and that I've let everyone from my pharmacist to my drug dealer down."

While insisting incidents such as this were rare, Olympic officials conceded that occurrences such as this one potentially undermine the Olympic ideals of cheating, greed and big business sponsorship and soon all everyone will be left with is a sporting event.

OLYMPIC GAMES

Exclusive to the Independent

Clive James

THE world's most famous Australian returns home to cover the event they call "Sydney 2000 Words".

Hedonism is the headline. This is the biggest party since Ned Kelly rode a kangaroo across Sydney Harbour and the young Clive James wanged his donger in the kedgeree. If you thought Australia was an old-fashioned place where blokes in funny hats throw Fosters on the barbie and down raw prawns by the tinnie then think again. The new Australia has become the greatest, happiest, most beautiful place to live in the world. That's why I live in England. *(Cont'd. p. 94)*

Exclusive to the Independent on Sunday and Sunday Telegraph

Kathy Lette

THE world's most famous Australian returns home to cover the event they call "Sydney 2000 Pounds".

Australians give good hedonism. In fact, they give the best hedonism in the world. They are way ahead on giving hedonism *(Get on with it. Ed.)*. Watching all those muscly athletes doing their stuff makes me want to join them in the breast stroke! Or the Phworr Hundred Metres! Or maybe the boys in the relay want to give me the Baton – all of them! Throw your javelin in my direction, mate! Is that a hammer in your lycra shorts or are you just pleased to see me?

The Australians certainly give great hedonism. That's why I live in England. *(Cont'd. p. 94)*

Exclusive to Everyone Else

Robert Hughes

THE world's most famous American returns home to cover the event they call "Sydney 2000 Expatriates Writing The Same Piece".

The Australian impulse towards the hedonistic is *(continued for ever)*

ARCHER TRIAL

Do you swear to tell the truth, the whole truth and nothing but the truth?

Don't be ridiculous

BRITAIN WINS OLYMPICS

by Our Sports Staff
Lunchbox O'Booze

IN THE most extraordinary and emotional games of all time, Britain's brave boys and girls took on the entire world and won. *(Are you sure? Ed.)*

In every sport the story was the same. From the Coxless Decathlon to the 400 Metre Volleyball, the plucky Brits faced the planet's best athletes and trounced them.

Amidst scenes of wild jubilation in the Olympic Stadium, the world's foreigners could only look on and marvel as Brit after Brit stepped up to hear the stirring strains of "The Stars and Stripes" (Surely "God Save The Queen"? Ed.) and even the partisan Aussie crowd cheered themselves hoarse as they acknowledged our total supremacy across the sporting board.

As the final tally of medals made crystal clear, Sydney 2000 will go down in history as the British Olympics. The figures speak for themselves:

1st: Britain — 11 Gold Medals

2nd: America — 39 Gold Medals

3rd: Russia — 32 Gold Medals

Last: France — Hardly any at all.

Late News

Top Olympic reporter Mr Lunchbox O'Booze was sent home in disgrace last night after failing a drugs test.

He admitted taking large quantities of a performance-enhancing substance (Vodka). He told IAAF officials, "I took the drug and suddenly the British performance was incredibly enhanced." *(Rotters)*

1ST WORLD

2ND WORLD

3RD WORLD

GLENDA SLAGG

A Personal Tribute to TV's Paula

SO the guttering candle that was the tragic Paula has finally been snuffed out. When I last saw her, she was rebuilding her life and coming off the drugs and the booze. She was proving to the world that she was at heart a truly caring, loving mother.

And now she has gone. And good riddance to her. The last thing you could call Paula was a caring, loving mother. When I last saw her, she had made no attempt to rebuild her life and was still on the drugs and the booze.

Yesterday the guttering candle was finally snuffed out. Surely now we should build a lasting memorial to the People's Paula — a dignified tribute to a woman who was famous for being famous and who, let's face it, does not deserve a memorial of any kind. © G. Slagg

CHURCHILL REVISITED

I have nothing to offer you but sweat

COMPLETELY WET

I need an aerosol

That's no way to talk about the Chancellor

Dr Thomas Utterfraud
Medical Opinion

As a doctor I am often asked to dash off a quick 1000 words on why people sweat (or Perspirato Nondeodorantensis, as we doctors call it).

The answer is very simple. Sweating is caused by a complete lack of policies, compounded by amnesia and an ability to admit that the Dome is a complete fiasco.

If you are worried about sweating, or that you have fallen behind in the opinion polls, you should consult a spin doctor at once. He will prescribe a change of shirt and your problem will be solved.

© *The Times.*

 BELGRADE TELEGRAPH

6 October 2000

BLAIROVIC REFUSES TO GO

by Our Political Staff **Bel Grade**   London, Tuesday

BRITAIN's embattled leader Swetalot Blairovic was last night desperately clinging to power in the face of mass public protest and an emphatic poll verdict calling for him to go.

Old-age pensioners and truckers linked arms and howled for Blairovic to step down and hand over to the opposition (Gordievski Brown).

SERPS

But his long-serving henchman Pyotr Mandelsonofabich told a mass rally of party members (Sid and Boris Blairovich) "Our leader is victorious regardless of what the electorate says."

However, one 190-year-old pensioner, Barbara Castle, disagreed. "It is time for this tyrant to depart. His shirt is stained with the sweat of downtrodden masses."

Blairovic is insisting on a second vote which he feels will give him time to regain the support of his once loyal people.

MILOSEVIC SAYS "I'M LISTENING"

Party leader Slobodan Milosevic today bounced back after his recent difficulties with a rousing conference speech, promising to kill anybody who opposed him. Shots rang out as (Cont'd. p. 94)

THE LATE DONALD DEWAR
An Apology

IN COMMON with all other newspapers, we may in recent years have given the impression that we entertained a low opinion of the late First Minister of Scotland.

Articles suggesting that the Scottish Parliament was a flop and a waste of money and that his brief stewardship of the Parliament was an unmitigated disaster. Headlines such as "Donald Dither – Time to Resign", "Donald – Where's Yer Policies?" and "Gang Awa' Back To London Yer Daft Donnie" (The Scotsman – prop. B. Pad) may have reinforced this impression.

We now accept that, on the contrary, Mr Dewar was a World Statesman of towering genius, whose legacy will be immortal and whose loss is incalculable:- see hundreds of articles this week headed "Donald Braveheart", "St. Donald of Scotland" and "Gang Awa' to Heaven ye Donnie Prince Dewar" (The Scotsman – prop. B. Pad).

On This Day: 2000

Führer What A Scorcher!

Angry crowds last night made a huge bonfire of thousands of new books about Adolf Hitler. "We've had enough of this poisonous filth," they chanted. "Surely authors have got something else to write about after 60 years of this stuff?" In the picture we see books by Ian Kershaw and Gitta Sereny being thrown on the fire to join all the others that (cont. p. 94)

Post-traumatic stress counsellor

HUNTER

10

LABOUR CONFERENCE

The pensioners are revolting

Speak for yourself, Worzel

SCHOOL UNIFORMS

PRINCE WILLIAM LASHES OUT IN TRAITOR FURY

by Our Royal Staff **Penny Judas**

IN AN amazing outburst of uncontrolled fury a seething Prince William viciously tore into the author of a controversial new book about his mother by a former aide.

He was asked by Royal reporter Reg Toady of the Mirror: "Would Your Highness care to comment on this disgusting book being serialised by a rival newspaper and would you agree that the author should be condemned to death."

William immediately snapped back, "Thank you all for coming. I shall be giving you details of my gap year in just a minute."

When pressed again on the subject by Julian Lackey of the Telegraph the Prince snarled, "I shall be spending much of my gap year under canvas." This is believed to be a reference to The Hon. Lavinia Canvas, 22, of Bangor.

That Gap Year In Full

1. William to visit Gap on Kings Road to purchase pair of combat trousers.

2. Er...

3. That's it.

LECTURER ACCUSED OF TEACHING STUDENT

by Our Education Staff **Alma Mater** and **Conrad Blackboard**

A 36-YEAR-OLD college lecturer was yesterday alleged to have engaged in regular "lectures and tutorial sessions" with girl students.

The court heard how the lecturer, who cannot be named (because we don't know who he is), had "written down all his students' names in a book".

Said Miss X, 19, "He is a disgrace to his profession. I went to his lectures, expecting to be molested, but instead he just talked about Hegel's theory of the dialectic."

The case continues.

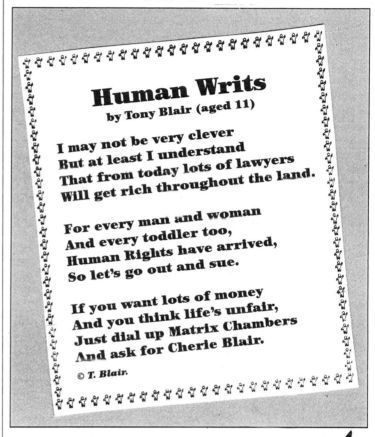

"Go to jail. Go indirectly to jail via the Court of Human Rights. Do not go to jail at all. Collect £200 million"

THOSE WERE THE KRAYS

He was the People's Murderer

CRIMINAL COURT CIRCULAR

The State Funeral of Sir Reginald Kray, Murderer to the Gentry and Knight Commander of the Order of the Diamond Geezer

That procession in full

1ST HEARSE
The late Lord Reginald Kray of Parkhurst GBH.

1ST MINICAB
Lady Roberta Kray, widow of the deceased and lady-in-waiting The Rt. Hon. Nosherina De Vorcee.

1ST STRETCH LIMOUSINE
Dame Barbara Windsor (representing the Queen Victoria pub), Sir Wayne Muscles (Toy-Boy Pursuivant) and smally fluffy dog, Crippen.

1ST STOLEN CAR
(FORD SIERRA COSWORTH)
Vince "The Hatchet" Gutterini, Dave "Piano Wire" Baird-Smith, Patrick "No Nickname" Maloney.

1ST POLICE CAR
The Rt. Hon. the Earl of Longford, Dame Myra Hindley of the Moors, Inspector "Knacker of the Yard" Knacker.

1ST COACH
Ron "Snapper" Filth (representing the Newspaper Industry), Mr John "Fastbuck" Blake (representing the Publishing Industry), Mr Guy "Madonna's husband" Ritchie (representing the British Gangster Film Industry).

APOLOGIES FOR ABSENCE
Mr Jack "The Hat" McVitie and various headless corpses buried in shallow graves around the Billericay area.

Pop Music Is Rubbish

by George Michael

IS IT me, or has popular music taken a turn for the worse recently? All we seem to get nowadays are manufactured boy bands who all sound the same, dress the same, and what's more – they even look the same! Record chiefs aren't interested in *real* talent anymore, all they want is pre-packaged pap which is aimed at the lowest common denominator. Speaking of which, the new Wham! Christmas compilation album will soon be on sale, featuring such memorable hits as: *Wake Me Up Before You Go Go, Club Tropicana* and many, many more. Anyway, where was I? Oh yes – Westlife, I mean, they've simply *got* to be miming, haven't they? And as for Boyz... *(cont. page 94)*

HAGUE 'NOT RACIST' SHOCK

Some of my best friends are rum and blacks

"THE BEST BRITISH FILM EVER" Daily Mail

Billy Hague

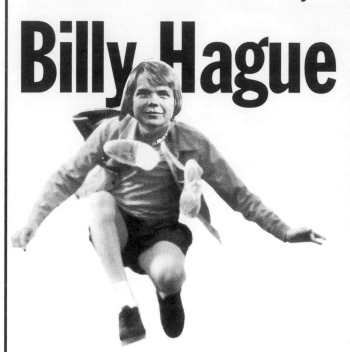

A touching story of a young Northern boy who defies his Yorkshire roots by becoming a young "Conservative". Shunned by all his friends, young Billy goes to London where he is adopted by a kind old lady with a handbag. She teaches him how to be a Conservative and turns him into a star, until he finally wins the supreme prize by being chosen for the role of leader of the Tory Party.

Billy	WAYNE SLEEP
Old Lady	DAME MARGARET FONTEYN
Michael Heseltine	RUDOLF NUREYEV
Tony Blair	LIONEL BLAIR

Eye Rating: *Ballet ridiculous*

NOT ANOTHER BLOODY SHIRT!

Letters to the Editor

Those Trafalgar Square Statues

SIR – So, Mr Ken Livingstone has never heard of General Sir Henry Havelock-Gussett (1809-97), the so-called "Saviour of the Hinduja Kush".

Well, let me tell Mr Livingstone that there are still plenty of us who still revere the memory of this great English patriot and soldier, who will be remembered long after the likes of Mr Livingstone and his newts are forgotten.

Havelock was my great-great-great crested newt (Surely "grandfather"?) and was venerated by generations of Punjabis, who knew him simply as "Gussett sahib". His relief of the siege of Hatterjee during the Mutiny was one of the finest feats of arms in the entire history of the British Empire, only equalled, may I suggest, by Mr Andrew Flintoff's sterling 83 in the more recent one-day siege of Karachi last week.

Sir Herbert Gussett
Dunsepoysin, Dorset

SIR – Much as Mr Livingstone would no doubt prefer to see his heroes Joseph Stalin and Che Guevarra commemorated in Trafalgar Square, many of us will continue to honour the memory of that illustrious diplomat, warrior and scholar Sir Hubert Dalrymple Gussett-Napier (1841-1910).

It was he of course who sent the famous telegram to Lord Palmerston bearing the single word "Avocado", which as every schoolboy knows is the Latin for "I have relieved the siege of Mafeking". Within minutes of the news arriving in London, bonfires were lit the length and breadth of the land and schoolchildren were handed a small cake known ever afterwards as a "Napier Bun".

No wonder Mr Livingstone wishes to sweep away thousands of years of British history, and put up instead statues of Lady Gavron and Peter Tatchell.

Brigadier The Rev Henry Napier-Gussett
Old Meldrew, Berks

SIR – Your correspondent Sir Henry Napier-Meldrew is quite wrong when he repeats the old chestnut of the "Avocado telegram". What Sir Hubert Gussett-Napier in fact cabled to the Foreign Office was "Fortunavo" – ie, "I am in luck now" – which the Latin scholars of the diplomatic corps immediately recognised as heralding the news that he had lifted the siege of Lucknow.

Sir Herbert Napier-Havelock
The Old Dome, Greenwich

SIR – My suggestion for two statues in Trafalgar Square would be Posh and Becks. She would "spice" up the Square, while he would "score" with all the tourists.

Mike Giggler
(Via e-mail)

SIR – Your readers may be interested to know about my train journey into London this morning. When I rang up at 3.45am to ascertain whether the River Carter Uck had subsided sufficiently to allow trains to resume service on the line between Ucknow and Charing Cross, I was told to "press the star button twice and (cont. p. 94)

The Book of Barak

Chapter One

1. And it came to pass in the days of Bar-ak that peace had come upon the land of Is-rael.

2. And when we speak of "peace", we speaketh only in relative terms.

3. And, lo, one of the children of Israel, named Ariel son of Sharon liketh not the peace between the children of Is-rael and the Arab-ites, the Araf-ites, the Hamas-ites, the Hezboll-ites and all the other-ites that dwell in the land that was once Pales-tine.

4. And Shar-on girded up his loins and went up unto Jer-u-salem, where he came unto the place that is holy to the Arab-ites, even the Dome of the Rock.

5. Then the Arab-ites saw Shar-on walking in their holy place as if he owneth it, and they did wax exceeding wroth.

6. And the Arab-ites spoke one to another, asking "Who among us will cast the first stone?"

7. And they cried out with one voice, "We all will."

8. Then they gathered up rocks from the ground and cast them at the sons of Is-rael.

9. And Bar-ak waxed even more wroth than the Arab-ites, and said "The sons of Ara-fat have asked for it this time. Let the smiting begin."

10. And so it came to pass. There was smiting throughout the land of Is-rael, and the sons of Go-liath, with their sling-stones, did not do very well against the sons of Dav-id, with their attack helicopters, armoured assault vehicles and heat-seeking missiles.

11. The score at the going down of the sun was as follows (and ye who wisheth not to knoweth the score may look away now): Children of Is-rael 112, Palestine 7.

12. And behold, in the midst of the smiting, there appeared unto both sides a vision, even of Clin-ton, he that cometh from the land of US and is called "the Maker of Peace".

13. And he calleth together Bar-ak and Ara-fat, that they might lay down their arms and fall upon each other's necks and pro-claim that from that day forth their two peoples would live in peace forever, even as the winged hornet lieth down with the mountain badger in the noonday sun.

14. And so it came to pass, in the town of Sharm-el-Sheikh, which is the Hebrew for "photo-opportunity".

15. But sadly when Ara-fat and Bar-ak returned each unto his own land, they found that their people were too busy casting stones and smiting to hear the great news that peace had come upon them.

16. And Ara-fat rent his towel, even the cloth that is on his head, and curseth Bar-ak, saying "Goeth ye, even unto hell."

17. Then Bar-ak cried aloud unto his people, "Who can doeth business with such an man? Let the smiting continue."

18. For it is the only language these people understand, even as the prophet Kabbi hath laid down.

19. And Bar-ak calleth unto Sharon saying, "Let us sit down together, you and I, even as the dove sitteth down with the hawk that eateth him for breakfast."

20. Then rose-up the Arab-ites and the Hezboll-ites and the Saddam-ites and all other-ites and cried "Let there be int-i-fada, which is to say war without end against the children of Israel."

21. And so it came to pass, even unto the ninety-fourth day.

SHADOW CABINET ADMIT EXPERIMENTING WITH CONSERVATISM

by Our Drugs Staff **Edward Du Cannabis** and **Marijuana Sieghart**

PRIVATE EYE has approached seven leading members of the Shadow Cabinet, who have confirmed that in their youth they all tried the drug "Conservatism", but did not like it.

This shock admission has gravely embarrassed the Tory leadership and in particular Miss Ann Widdecombe who is known to be a conservative addict who likes "the strong stuff" and was last week hailed as the "heroin" of the Tory conference.

What They Told The Eye

Oliver Nitwit, 29, shadow minister for paperclips.
"Yes, I once tried it at university. We called it 'Thatch' in those days. But it was too strong for me."

David Spriggett, 31, shadow spokesman for e-commerce.
"Yes, I gave it a go when I was 17. But nothing happened, and I just felt a bit silly and talked a lot of rubbish for a while."

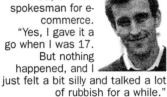
Lord Spliffclyde, 48, shadow leader of the Lords select committee on proportional representation.
"I was never really hooked on it, but we all did a bit of it in the 80s. 'Maggijuana', that's what we used to call it."

Peter Jobsworth, 46, shadow minister for something or other.
"I admit I tried it once, but it was a long time ago. You grow out of that sort of thing."

Francis Fraude, 49, shadow of his former self.
"I met this man at a Spectator party called Enoch. He was clearly on something pretty amazing. It was heady stuff. But unfortunately when I tried it I was sick."

Bernard Junkey, 34, shadow spokesman for eye shadow.
"Who gave you my number, you bastards! I bet it was that bugger Potillo."

Charles Mooruana, 22, shadow editor of the Daily Telegraph.
"I tried it when I was a schoolboy, and you could say I'm hooked for life. It doesn't do you any harm, quite the opposite. In fact, it's like permanently living in another world. You feel relaxed all the time. You just want to chill out and put naked birds on the front page all the time."

Barbara Amiel-Nitrate, shadow wife of the proprietor of the Daily Telegraph.
(That's enough confessions of former Toryheads. Ed.)

NO ASYLUM SEEKERS

---

8 HOURS THAT SHOOK THE WORLD

by Our Yugoslavia Staff **Phil Space**

NO ONE expected it and when it happened the sheer speed of events caught everyone by surprise. On the Wednesday morning it was business as usual. But within eight hours life would never be the same again.

Here is the Extraordinary Timetable of Events.

10.17 Editor notices Sky News report that Milosevic has been ousted.

10.18 Editor rushes into newsroom and gives me 8 hours to fill 12 pages full of stuff about Yugoslavia.

10.19 Ditch analysis feature about Sophie Dahl ("Is fat the new thin?").

10.25 Storm the cuttings library and present list of demands. (Who is Milosevic? What is Serbia? Is there a football angle?)

2.15 Discover that I wrote huge piece in May headlined "The Dictator They Will Never Topple".

2.17 Hold rally with subs in pub. Agree strategy of big pictures and enormous graphics.

4.20 Abandon pub and launch all-out attack on key internet sites.

5.34 Seize downloaded article from Professor of Balkan studies at the University of Didcot (formerly the British School of Motoring).

6.17 Triumphantly hand in 10,000 words with headline "What a Load of Balkans".

■ THE GEOGRAPHY OF TERROR ■

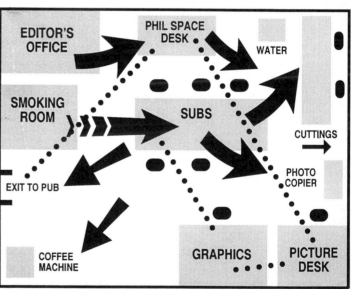

FAT OLD MAN RETIRES

by Our Entire Staff **Phil Pages**

A FAT old man yesterday announced that he was retiring.

Now aged 84, the Fat Old Man has been in the same job for 50 years.

(Reuters)

ON OTHER PAGES
Picture special "The Fat Old Man when he was a fat young man" **2, 3, 4, 5**
The Fat Old Man's hobbies **6, 7, 8, 94**

NOT ON OTHER PAGES
Fat Old Man's links with Chinese Money and loony cults.

SUPERMODELS

KERBER

POETRY CORNER

**In Memoriam Ted Rogers,
Quiz Show Host**

So. Farewell then
Ted Rogers.

3-2-1.

Yes, that
Was your
Catchphrase.

And Dustybin –
He was your
Co-star.

3-2-1.

Yes. You
Are in the
Dustybin
Of History.

E.J. Thribb (3-2-17½)

**Lines On The 80th Birthday
of Mr Humphrey
"Humph" Lyttleton**

So. Congratulations
Humphrey Lyttleton.

Band leader and
Radio quiz show host.

Bad Penny Blues.
That was your
Hit.

Yes, we remember
How it goes –
Da da di da
Di da da
(Repeat)

But what was
Your long-running
Programme called?

I'm sorry I
Haven't a Clue[1]

E.J. Thribb (17½)

[1]**Andrew Motion* writes**
Once again Thribb shows his verbal dexterity by
providing a final three-line stanza with a double
meaning, leaving the reader in a state of what
Keats called "Heightened Ambiguity."

*Andrew Motion's latest work *Lines To Miss
Laura Fish* is in the possession of the relevant
authorities. The Eye can however reveal the
opening verse of the collection: *Ms Laura
Fish/You are a dish/But don't make any trouble/
Or you'll be out at the double.*

WE'RE HERE FOR ALL ETERNITY!

STILL, MUSN'T GRUMBLE

Those Pantsdown Diaries In Full

Continuing the Times's exclusive serialisation of the most sensational political document since the autobiography of Norman Fowler

Jan 17th 1997: Tony asked me to come round to his place for a "secret session". This is the big one! Tonight I feel I am really going to score! Tony greets me at the door. he is wearing tight Levis, a lovely blue shirt from Hawkshead (£9.95) and some groovy own-brand trainers from Asda (£13.99). He led me down into the cellar with a conspiratorial wink. "We don't want anyone to see us, particularly Gordon!" he said. "I've been thinking," he went on, "about what you said last Tuesday. But I'm not sure we really want to be going quite so far down that particular road. I'm just not ready for it, as of now." I felt curiously disappointed, not to mention frustrated. When we spoke before, he seemed so positive, so committed. Surely he couldn't be thinking of stringing me along and then dumping me, could he?

May 1st 1997 Disaster! The News of the World has found out about me and Tony! They've got all the lurid details – times, places, who said what to whom, even our private messages! I rang Tony on our special private line. "Ashdown?" I heard his familiar voice asking. "I think you must have a wrong number. I've never heard of Mr Ashdown and I'm a happily married man. Ask my wife, Gordon."

© *Lord Pantsdown of Yeovil 2000.*

Tomorrow: My poor wife Jane is really hurt when she finds out about my affair. I am so sorry I write it all up in my diary and get it published in the Times so everyone can read it again.

TV Highlights

Wildlife

The Mating Habits of the Salmon (BBC)

DAVID Attenborough introduces fascinating footage showing the ex-head of BBC1, Mr Peter Salmon, leaping up the skirt *(Surely "stream"?)* of gorgeous, pouting Coronation Street barmaid Racquel in order to lay his actress *(Surely "eggs"?)*. Attenbore comments, "I have never seen anything like these scenes. Nothing like this would have happened when I was head of BBC2 back in the Sixties."

Comedy

One Foot in The Gravy (BBC1)
PETER Salmon is being paid £300,000 to be Head of Sport. But wasn't he dumped from his job as Controller of BBC1 because the Channel was so bad? Laughs all round from the licence payer.

New from BBC Sport

11.45 Horizontal Jogging from White City
12.15 Second Leg(over) of the F.U. Cup
1.00 Bedroom Olympics live from Uganda

Science

The Human Body: The Miracle of the Moustache (BBC)

FEW phenomena have baffled medical science as much as the growth of hair on the upper lip of Lord Winston.

What on earth is the point of it? Tonight we go inside the moustache and watch the individual follicles emerging in high-speed stopframe motion to create a luxuriant growth underneath his nose.

And finally we discover the secret purpose of the moustache.

To give everyone a good laugh on a Sunday night.

DO YOU HAVE ANYTHING TO REMOVE THE LIMESCALE FROM TAPS?

HAMPSTEAD STORE

FILIPINO?

𝕲nome

GNOME Newspapers are proud to announce that they have secured the services of the internationally-renowned cookery and lifestyle expert, Gnomella Gnome.

Gnomella will be providing her cooking tips exclusively to readers of the Daily Gnome and the Gnome on Sunday, showing how the working woman of today can still be a domestic goddess. This is the first recipe for you to cut out and keep – unless you are too busy.

Recipe Number One
Children's Tea

Fish Fingers

Fish fingers make a delightful tea-time treat for kids. I find the best way to prepare them is to buy them in the supermarket and read the cooking instructions on the back.

Garnish with tomato ketchup (don't bother with home-made – I find Heinz is perfectly acceptable!) and serve.

NEXT WEEK: How to buy biscuits.

WHO ARE THEY?
– The Great And Good Who Make Up The Runnynose Commission, Authors Of *Britain Don't You Hate It? The Future of Multiculture*

CHAIR

Lord Hoohi, lecturer in anti-British studies at the University of Humberside (formerly Grimsby Polytechnic).

VICE-CHAIR

Lady Horlicks, wife of very rich owner of The Express and former commissioning editor for Channel Four's landmark documentary series "Britain – Land of Nazis".

MEMBERS

Andrew Mars-Bar, formerly political editor of the Indescribablyboring, now BBC's Chief Blair Correspondent.

Mrs Pashmina Ali-Baba Brown, columnist on racial discrimination for the Racial Discrimination Section of The Indescribablyboring.

Sir Mohammed Uzzi, reader in Anti-Imperialist Studies, University of Bermondsey (formerly the Star of India, Tooley Street).

Sir Tariq Noodle, chair of the Committee to promote Inter-Racial Harmony in the Race Relations Industry.

Mr Ephraim O'Hardcastle, director of the Centre for Irish-Jewish Studies, Hexham.

Professor Adolf Wong, Lecturer in Positive State Censorship at the Chow Mein Kampf Institute, Sunningdale.

Lady Gavroche, wife of very rich owner of The Guardian and friend of Mr Blair. *(That's enough ridiculous people. Ed.)*

Mr Jack Straw – A Statement

Mr Jack Straw, the Home Secretary, wishes to make clear after reading adverse press comment on the above, that he had nothing whatever to do with the Runnyegg Report which is now all over his face.

Mr Straw is proud to be British and has no intention of implementing a report which he merely commissioned and promised to implement.

Cowboy Empire Builders

"Colonise Central Africa? Now you're asking. OK, cash in hand. Darren'll be in Mombasa Monday or Tuesday..."

That Runnymede Trust History Of The Country Formerly Known As Britain

1948 AD BRITAIN first discovered by Afro-Caribbean explorers on their ship the Empire Windrush.

1950s Many black settlers arrive in the islands and establish colonies in Notting Hill, Brixton and the NHS.

1960s First Indian restaurants established.

1968 Second wave of Asian settlers from East Africa complete "civilising mission" by opening thousands of corner-shops.

1970s First mosques built in Regents Park and Bradford. Many natives converted led by Cat Stevens, and later Jemima Kahn (daughter of Sir James Puddleduck).

1985 Famous battle of Broadwater Farm, ends in total victory for Generals Bernie Grant and Sir Winston Silcott.

1997 Tony Blair leads multi-ethnic coalition to historic triumph in General Election.

2000 Runnymede Trust publishes ridiculous report, leading to increased racial tension and outbreaks of general bad feeling.

POLLY FILLER

IF I hear another boring middle-class woman droning on at a dinner party about her children's education I'm going to scream! Aaargh!

Why don't these women realise that we've all been there, done that and bought the school blazer from John Lewis! (Or rather waited for weeks for the stupid girl in John Lewis' useless uniform department to organise its delivery! For an outrageous £75 I don't expect to have to send the au pair to collect it!)

What these "school bores" won't get into their silly heads is that I don't want to hear about how little India would have gone to state school, but it wasn't good enough and she had to go to the local independent prep... zzzzz! Honestly!

In our case, of course, there *was* no choice. I genuinely wanted Charlie to get a proper social mix at a state school, but our local primary is only 14th in the National SATS League Table and we agonised about whether we had the right to inflict our conscience on our toddler. Even the useless Simon stirred himself from Naked Pro-Celebrity Taekwondo from Ottowa on Channel 5 to look round some pre-preps with me. Millhouse has a lovely atmosphere, St Reginald's is good for games and the Tweazles have kids reading French by four and a half! Impressive, eh?

Yes, we felt we were betraying our principles. Yes, we were letting down the state system. And, yes, I could pay the school fees if I knuckled down and wrote a couple of columns.

So, Charlie starts at the Plank School next year because he is borderline dysmotoproxic. (Aren't all men?)

But who wants to hear about this stuff? Not me! So, if you're seated next to me at dinner please keep your dreary education sagas to yourself! Or you're likely to get a spoonful of Nigella's Pea Risotto in your face!!

Next week: How Charlie's first week at school drove her to take up smoking again.

"I think we should defer Arthur's test until a later date"

BSE INQUIRY
Guilty named

Daisy, Buttercup, Clover, Cowslip

BSE REPORT – New victim

by Our Mad Cow Disease Staff **Lunchtime O'Moos**

THE Government has issued a warning to the public to avoid any contact with the "Phillips Report", commonly known as "Mad Mandarin's Disease".

Those who have swallowed it have complained of feelng confused and disorientated. Said one victim, "It's terrible. After only a couple of pages I didn't know what I thought any more."

Tasteless

Experts say that the Government knew all along what the report contained, but still did nothing to stop it being freely available to the general public.

Now that the Report is in the chain, there are fears that it will contaminate *(Continued p. 94)*

STORMS LATEST

I offer you my resignation

SOMETHING IN BRITAIN WORKS SHOCK

by Our Incompetence Staff **John Bulls-Up**

THE ENTIRE country was in a state of shock last night when it was revealed that something in Britain was working normally.

There were immediate calls for a full judicial enquiry to look into the reasons behind this latest emergency. "It is a national disgrace," said one commentator, "that something in Britain should have been allowed to function without going disastrously wrong and ruining the lives of millions of people." He continued, "What is wrong with us that we cannot stop something like this happening?"

(Rotters)

Radio Four, Today programme

...which I think rules out Venables.

Sue McGhastly: Thank you, Garry. And now the news headlines.

Man With Beard *(B. Perkins, for it is he)*: There's been a rail crash near Hatfield. The cause of the crash is not yet known, and a spokesman for Railtrack said, "It's too early to speculate."

McGhastly: Thank you, Brian. As you rightly say, it's too early to speculate as to the reasons for this dreadful disaster, but let's go over live to our reporter Phil Time who is sitting next to me here in the studio.
Phil, I know it's too early to speculate...

Phil: That's right, Sue, it's too early to speculate.

McGhastly: But nevertheless, I wonder if we can begin to work out why this terrible accident might have happened. I mean, could it have been terrorism?

Phil: That's right, Sue, although Railtrack are still saying that it's too early to speculate. That's the message we're getting from Railtrack at this moment in time.

McGhastly: Well, the crash could alternatively have been down to driver error.

Phil Time: Indeed it could, Sue. But right now the message from Railtrack is that it really is too early to speculate.

McGhastly: What about a giant fireball crashing to earth from outer space hurling hundreds of bodies into the air? I know it's too early to come to any definite conclusions, but would that fit with the evidence we have so far?

Phil Time: That's a good point, Sue, and I'm sure that is one of the possibilities the enquiry will be looking into.

McGhastly: Well, I'm sure we'll be returning to that after the news, and possibly by that time we'll have a proper body count. But now it's Thought For The Day with the Chief Druid.

E.F. Harbottle, Chief Druid: You know, when I heard the news just now of this train that has been destroyed by an atomic fireball near Hatfield, my thoughts immediately went out to all the emergency services, many of whom I am sure are practising druids...

James Naughtie: And I'm sorry to interrupt you, Chief Druid, but news is just coming in that a record £250,000 advance has been offered to Sue McGhastly for her memoirs. Sue, I know it's too early to speculate, but do you think honestly anyone is going to buy your book?

John Humphrys *(for it is he)*: Come on, admit it, Sue, it'll be just a load of boring anecdotes about sitting round this table drinking BBC coffee and listening to the Chief Druid...

Chief Druid: When I heard the news about this record advance for Sue, my heart went out to all the thousands of people who might be bored to death by reading it, and I felt *(Cont'd. KHz 94)*

A _sandbag_?

BIRCH

VERY IMPORTANT ANNOUNCEMENT

From Virgin First Great Sweetex North East

Due to factors beyond our control, the following revised timetable will operate until May 3 2006 (subject to revision).

Railtrack PLC

Table 94a

London, Paddington	dep	0723	0738	0750	0753	......	0805
Mowlam Junction	dep	0730	0742	0745	0757	......	0815
Massingberd-Super-Mare	dep	......	0748	......	......	0818	......
Beckham	dep	......	......	......	0812	0832	......
Ashdown	dep	0744	0757	......	0814	0827	0844
Birmingham New Street	dep	0802	0819	0829	0832	0846	0849
Birmingham Old Street	dep	0802	......	0822	......	0832	0852
Coronation Street	dep	0807	0829	......	0837	0859	......
Gregdyke Parkway	dep	0814	......	0850	......	0920	......
Hurley Central	dep	0820	0850	......	0920	0926	0929
West Frostrup	arr	0858	......	0908	0927	......	......
East Frostrup	dep	0903	......	0913	0932	......	0943
Karachi Central	dep	......	0900	......	0913	0918	0923
Widdecombe	arr	0907	0925	0930	......	0937	0940

a. Mowlam Junction is closed due to flooding. A bus service to Stroud and Gloucester will operate on Wednesdays between 0045 and 0615 hrs (except on Wednesdays).

b. All trains to Ashdown are cancelled until further notice. Passengers are advised to seek other means of transport.

c. For safety reasons, speed restrictions will be in force between Gregdyke Parkway and Hurley Central between 0725 and 0724 hrs. The speed limit approved by the Health and Safety Executive will be 0 mph.

d. The Westlife Express between Beckham and Ashdown North (not advertised) will commence its journey at Redwood until January 24. It will then go forward via Althorp Park, Portillo East and St Petersburg, to terminate somewhere in the Gobi Desert. The service will be running approximately 45 minutes late.

e. Coaches to form the 1427 stopping train from Stothard to Wapshott will divide at Tonbridge, due to a collapse of the track. The first two coaches will continue under water to Lewes and all stations to Atlantis North. The rear three coaches will burst into flames.

f. Owing to adverse weather conditions, it will not be possible to provide customer information of any kind, except on the internet at www.notrains.com.muta

g. Customers are warned that the railway companies are in no way responsible for the running of the train services, and that any customer daring to ask staff about the timing or destination of trains will face prosecution (maximum penalty £50,000 or five years imprisonment).

For the well-being of customers, all our trains operate a non-running policy. (Surely non-smoking? G. Corbett).

THOMAS
THE PRIVATISED TANK ENGINE

THOMAS was unhappy about the mess the Fat Controller had made of the Railway. "Why don't you do the decent thing?" said Thomas. "Very well," said the Fat Controller and he threw himself in front of a train.

But of course there weren't any trains. Crafty old Fat Controller!

PRESCOTT REASSURES THE NATION

Trains are completely safe – I'd let my daughter eat one

THE GUARDIAN

Dumb?

A poll commissioned by the Guardian has revealed startling gaps in the cultural knowledge of young British adults – with this in mind, we raise the question of whether Britain is a nation in irreversible cultural decline. In a serious attempt to address these and other related issues, the Guardian invites you to check out its totally wicked new magazine, which features an in-depth interview with Fatboy Slim, a brilliant Lara Croft wallposter – *plus* all the very latest soap gossip. Sorted!

'Standards Are Appalling' Says Woodhead

BY OUR EDUCATION STAFF
LUNCHTIME O'FSTED

IN A sensational attack on his new employee, former schools inspector Chris Woodhead yesterday claimed that standards at the Daily Telegraph had been "allowed to fall far below an acceptable national level".

"I was shocked when I arrived at the Telegraph," he said, "to find that most of the journalists were illiterate, lazy and incompetent."

Conrad Blackboard

"The whole paper," Mr Woodhead continued, "reeks of half-baked, wishy-washy Sixties culture instead of the traditional values that the paper used to stand for.

"I was appalled," he said, "to see pictures of half-dressed women all over the news pages,

feeble interviews with pop stars on the arts pages and blatant propaganda for legalising marijuana in the editorials."

Mr Woodhead said that he put the blame for the collapse in standards firmly on the shoulders of the Telegraph's editor, Mr Charles Moore, whom he accused of being "weak and ineffectual."

Evening Standards

"It is all jolly unfair," said Mr Moore. "Everyone here is doing the best they can, in very difficult circumstances with limited resources.

"We have no canteen and have to work in a rundown docklands environment."

Mr Woodhead, however, is unrepentant and plans to send in a "hit squad" from the Times to restore confidence in the "sink" newspaper.

SHOULD THE BARCLAY TWINS BE SEPARATED?

asks Eye Medical Correspondent **Dr Thomas Utterfraud**

IN A delicate operation lasting 30 seconds, Her Majesty The Queen tried to separate the world-famous Barclay twins, who have been joined together since birth by a huge pile of money.

Both twins are said to be "comfortably off" said a spokesman.

Fleet Street's Anne Robinson

ANNE ROBINSON – aren'tchasickofher with her granny glasses, crooked mouth and 'orrible red hair!?!?! Who do you think your are??? Torquemada??!?! More like Torquerubbish!?!?! Who's the weakest link?? You are, you old bag!!!!?? No offence, Annie!!??!

ANNE ROBINSON – hats off to Annie Robinson!!?! The BBC's brilliant answer to Chris Tarrant!! Isn't it just great to see a middle-aged hackette suddenly become famous and get given a whole load of money!?!?! Are you listenin', Mr TV Producer??!?! I'm

free!!? And I could be the strongest link!!?!

HERE THEY ARE – Glenda's Pre-Christmas Cuddlies!!?!

Lord Hollick – With his little beard and twinkly eyes he can flog me anytime!!?!

Gerald Corbett (Mr Railtrack as was) – We'll take it slowly, Gerald, and put safety first!!?!? Geddit??!?!

Gobichand Hinduja – Crazee name, crazee guy!!?!?!

Byeeeeee!

THAT JOHN MORTIMER-AT-100 INTERVIEW IN FULL

by Philippa Page

A Private Eye Digest Service

YOU would never think he is 100. When we meet at the Ivy, he is already sitting in his favourite seat.

"Let's have some champers, shall we? It's awfully naughty, isn't it?" says the twinkly-eyed QC turned playwright, of the immortal Rumpole...

"...can't do up my shoelaces

any more..." "...still fancy a spot of the other at 100..." "...twinkle in his eye..." "more champagne, darling..." "...can't get my socks off..." "...new book coming out next week..." "as dear Johnny Gielgud once told me..." "...wife goes fox-hunting... blind father... agreeable house in Chilterns... New Labour... Blair very disappointing... more champagne... which one are you?"

© All national newspapers.

TV Film Choice

Goodbye Mr Woodhead
(1947) *(Black and White)*

CLASSIC British tearjerker, with dedicated teacher Mr Woodhead who falls in love with one of his sixth formers and has to leave. Robert Donat stars as Woodhead with James Robertson Justice as David Blunkett.

"You are the weakest link, goodbye"

EINSTEIN: THE NEW FACE OF BUDWEISER

"WAZZZZAA!"

The cleverest little pig built something that even the big bad wolf wouldn't bother visiting

Those 'Who Wants To Be A Millionaire?' Questions In Full

Eleanor of Aquitaine

These are the 10 questions that Mrs Judith Keppel answered on her way to becoming TV's first toff millionaire.

1. Of which city is Fulham a district?
A. Paris B. New York C. Helsinki D. London

2. Who is Prince Charles's mistress?
A. Julie Burchill B. Denise van Outen C. Anne Robinson D. Your cousin.

3. Is Peter Jones
A. A Welsh singer B. An Arsenal footballer C. A character in Emmerdale D. A place where you do your shopping.

4. Which popular BBC character is on the other channel at this moment?
A. Captain Mainwaring B. Tony Hancock C. Victor Meldrew D. Basil Fawlty.

5. When you win a million pounds would you like to take a holiday in
A. Torremolinos B. Butlins C. Provence D. Benidorm.

So we consign to the flames Algernon Dixon, fireworks salesman...

OOOOH! AAAAH!

NEW EUROPEAN ARMY – HOW IT WILL LOOK

'THE EURO-ARMY IS NOT A EURO-ARMY' Says Blair

by Our Political Staff
Yuri Phile

A FURIOUS Prime Minister last night lashed out at reports that Britain was signing up to an integrated European army.

"It is outrageous," said Mr Blair, "that these right-wing Europhobic journalists like Lord Owen, Lord Healey and Lord Carrington should go round spreading these hysterical lies about our purely pragmatic decision to create an integrated European army."

Hot Blair

"Nothing could be more unpatriotic," he continued, "than to oppose the armed wing of the single European currency, which is all that is on the table.

"And besides," Mr Blair concluded, "the not-the-European army would only be used in humanitarian emergencies, like the day when it becomes necessary for Europe to declare war on the United States of America.

"It is high time," screamed Mr Blair, his voice rising several octaves in his excitement, "that we Europeans demonstrate that we are a super-power capable of taking on anyone in the world – so long as the Americans give us the equipment."

That Non-European Army – How It Will Work

1. The RAF will in future be known as the Luftwaffe.
2. The Ark Royal will be renamed the Tirpitz.
3. The role of General Sir Peter de la Billiere will be played by Max von Sydow.
4. The 17/21st Kings Own Lancers will merge with the Danish Peace Corps, to become the European Housing Agency.
5. The England football team will be commanded by Field-Marshal Sven-Göran Eriksson.
6. The Imperial War Museum is to be renamed the Metric War Museum in accordance with EC Directive 80/181.
7. Regimental mascot for the European Rapid Reaction Force will be the snail.
8. The new motto for the British Army will be "For EU, Tommy, the war is over."
9. ...er...
10. ...that's it.

U.S. ELECTIONS
FINAL RESULTS

Bush $100,000,819
Gore $100,000,204

The Democrats have called for a recount after final figures showed George Bush edging ahead of Al Gore in the race to buy the Presidency of the United States.

CLOSEST U.S. ELECTION IN HISTORY

Maybe I shouldn't have voted for the other guy

TORTOISE AND HARE — TOO CLOSE TO CALL

by Our Race Staff **E. Sopp**

MR GEORGE W. Tortoise was last night awaiting confirmation as winner of the most extraordinary race in the history of fables.

In the early hours of the morning it looked as if Mr Al Hare had won and the American TV networks declared him the victor. But as the hours ticked by it appeared that Mr Tortoise, often criticised for being a bit slow, had in fact pulled off a remarkable comeback.

The pundits then declared Mr Tortoise as the overall champion only to find that Mr Hare had woken up and staged a dramatic last minute dash for the line.

Hare Brained

Finally, as dawn broke on the 94th day of the race, the organisers declared that there was indeed a loser – America.

THAT CONFUSING FLORIDA BALLOT PAPER IN FULL

(DEMOCRATIC REPUBLICAN PARTY) **GEORGE W. GUSH**	(REPUBLICAN DEMOCRATIC PARTY) **AL BORE**
(INDEPENDENT THIRD PARTY) **RALPH NADIR**	(NON-INDEPENDENT PRO-MURDOCH PARTY) **PAT BUCASSHOLE**
(AMERICAN SOCIALIST WORKERS PARTY) **DAVE SPARTMAN**	(MONSTER HAMBURGER RAVING PARTY) **SCREAMING LORD SUTCHBURGER III**

INSTRUCTIONS

Punch one hole only – i.e. that belonging to brother of Jebenezer Gush, Governor of the State of Florida (no relation)

PRESIDENT CLINTON
An Apology

IN RECENT years, in common with all other newspapers, we may have given the impression that President William Jefferson Clintstone III was without question the worst President in the entire history of the United States. Headlines such as "Sleazeball Clinton In New Sex Scandal", "Impeach President Liar Now", "Did Clinton Personally Order Slaying Of JFK As Part Of Nixon Whitewatergate Cigar Conspiracy?" may have led readers to think that we in some way felt that President Clinton was unworthy of the high office of chief executive.

Having seen these two new guys we now realise that President Clinton is undoubtedly the greatest President in the history of the United States and a political genius without parallel, who has been personally responsible for the economic miracle that has made America the happiest and most blessed nation since records began. We apologise for any confusion this may have caused to our readers and agree to pay our columnists even more money to get it wrong in future.

MEET THE CLINTSTONES – THE PREHISTORIC FIRST FAMILY

QUITE FAMOUS WOMAN MARRIES REALLY FAMOUS MAN

A woman who is quite famous was yesterday married to a really famous man.

Said a wedding guest, "They're almost the perfect match – what with him being really famous, and her being not-quite-so-famous."

How They Are Related

Catherine Zeta Jones

Michael Douglas

Alpha Jones	Spartacus
Beta Jones	Van Gogh
Gamma Jones	Captain James T. Kirk
Jones, the Baker	General Douglas McArthur
Jones, the Steam	Kirk Douglas
Jones, the Tom	Douglas DC-10
Jones, the Zeta	Douglas, Isle of Man
Jones, the Marry A Rich American Film Star	Michael Douglas

"Oh yeah... Since she married the prince, Snow White has really let herself go"

KES.

"I am not going to be bullied by the protestors into making concessions."

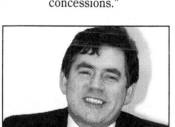

"I am going to do it voluntarily!"

NORTH CIRCULAR

14 November: The state visit of the People's Fuel Lobby took place in London today. A procession was formed as follows:

1st Lorry
Mr David "Dave" Yorkie and his son, Dave "Little Dave" Yorkie Junior.

1st Tractor
Farmer Giles Witherington-Spoon and his collie dog, Barker.

1st Long Vehicle
Mr Eddie Lager and his partner Mollie Sarnie.

Also in 1st Long Vehicle
60 illegal immigrants from Bangladesh.

1st Television Van
The BBC Points South West Traffic Update Team presenters Tricia Spangle and Mike Cone.

(That's enough procession. Ed.)

Those Deep-Vein Thrombosis Life-Threatening Long-Haul Journeys In Full

British Airways (London to Sydney)	20 hours
Japan Airlines (London to Tokyo)	14 hours
Connex South Central (London to Brighton)	37 hours

That Buckingham University Honorary Degree Citation In Full

SALUTAMUS DENISUM THATCHERENSIS, CONSORTUM FIDELUS PER MULTOS ANNOS MARGARETUM THATCHI (DUX SUPREMUS UNIVERSUS ET IMPERATRIX BRITTANIUM ET VICTOR FALKLANDI APPELLATU "FEMINA FERRUS" ET CETERA ET CETERA). BIBULUS MAXIMUM MULTOS SNORTOS TINCTUROSQUE GINUM ET TONICUS FAVORITUM PATER GEMINI MARCUS TWITTUS ET CAROLI SWEETICUS ET AMICUS SCRIBULI TELEGRAPHICO W.F. DEEDUSH (NOTABILE "SHURUS SHUMUS ERRATUM EST?"). MILLIONARUS ET POLITICUS EXTREMUS DEXTER VIZ HANGUM FLOGGUM ET STRINGUM UPQUE. HONORAMUS TE DENIS DOCTORE ARS PISSICUS!

© Buckingham University (formerly Ratners, Milton Keynes)

DAILY SEXPRESS

Friday December 1, 2000

PORN BARON SCREWS RIVALS OVER BEAVER PAPERS!

by SARAH SHANNON
Media Correspondent

RICHARD "Big Dick" Desmond has forked out £125 million to add the Soaraway Daily Sexpress and its sizzling sister Sunday to his bulging porn to porn media empire.

Says Dirty Desmond, "Blimey! I've scored here! What a couple of beauties I've got! I'm just the man to get it up – the circulation, I mean!"

Are You Getting It Daily?

Raunchie Rosie – Is she good for the sack? **3** **Rupert Bare** – The naughty naked cartoon hero has some adult fun at the nude Teddy Bears' Picnic! **5** **Your saucy stars tonight** – Virgo in Uranus with Jonathan Caner **7** Readers' Wives' Letters **9** **Whither the Euro** by political editor Anthony Bevins *(You're fired. R.D.)* **Has Britain gone to the dogs?** by Peter Hitchens *(You're fired as well. R.D.)*

"Ooer, this has never happened to me before"

RAIL PASSENGER TO RECEIVE COMPENSATION

by Our Rail Staff **Kay Oss**

IT WAS yesterday revealed that the compensation programme for those worst hit by recent rail chaos has begun, with Railtrack handing over a sum of £1 million to their biggest passenger, a Mr Gerald Corbett.

A spokesman for Mr Corbett said, "To qualify for his pay-out, Mr Corbett was required to sign a piece of paper saying, 'I'm rubbish, I quit.' As a consequence, Railtrack were more than happy to reimburse Mr Corbett with a generous sum of other people's money – which is roughly the equivalent to his yearly season ticket to The Seychelles, via the Gatwick Express."

The Number One Best-Seller
THE RAILTRACK BOOK OF RECORDS

compiled by Horace, Maurice and Boris McCorbett

Did you know that:

★The slowest train journey in history was the 7.42 Connex South East from East Grinstead to West Grinstead. It took 147 hours and 12 minutes!

★The world's shortest train was the 17.41 Virgin InterCity from Carlisle to Newcastle which had only enough room for the driver and guard!

★The most number of passengers in a single compartment was recorded on the 9.03 Thames Turbo Express from Bristol Temple Meads to Didcot Parkway. A staggering 12,642 customers crammed into the 2nd Class compartment!

★Mr Thomas Winterbottom, a 52-year-old civil servant managed to read the entire works of Anthony Powell during his week-long journey from Haywards Heath to Brighton.

★All these and many more amazing facts provide the best holiday entertainment for all the family who can't get home because there aren't any trains.

Modern Nursery Rhymes No. 94

Old Macdonald had a train.
E-I-E-I-O.

And on that train there were 2,000 people (because the previous three had been cancelled).
E-I-E-I-O.

With a "Hello darling, I'm on the train" here, and
A "Hello darling, I'm still on the train" there,
Everywhere a "This is disgraceful, I'm going to write to the Times",
Lord Macdonald had a job.
Y-O-Y-O-Y?

PORNOGRAPHER OWNS NATIONAL NEWSPAPER SHOCK!

Mmm... Asian babes!

IN THE COURTS

The Case of Sir Elton Spangle v. Bob Sponge (or it may be the other way round).

Day 94. The case continued before Mr Justice Cocklecarrot, in which popular singer Sir Elton Spangle (real name Reginald Nozzer) is suing his former manager and partner Mr Robert Sponge (real name Robert Sponge) for reasons that have not yet become clear.

Sir Hartley Redface Q.C. *(representing himself)*: We now come to the vexed matter of the 200 boxes of fox-fur underwear which the accused claims that he was given as a Saint Valentine's Day gift by Sir Spangle. Sir Spangle, is it not true that three and a half million pounds is a great deal of money to pay for what are no more than articles of gentleman's underclothing, be they scented with lavender or no?

Sir Elton Spangle: I frequently spend millions of pounds on knickers. But I do not keep a record of how much they actually cost. That's what people like Spongey are for.

Mr Sponge *(interrupting)*: Ooh, Miss High-and-Mighty! Hark at her! And the books weren't all I used to do for Spangles, I can tell you!

Mr Justice Cocklecarrot: You will have your chance, Mr Sponge, to tell us all. In the meantime, perhaps you would be so good as to allow Sir Hartley to continue. When it comes to expensive briefs, I think he is the expert!

(All lawyers collapse in hysterical laughter at this extraordinary example of judicial wit. The court adjourned for luncheon. Following the adjournment, Mr Sponge was recalled to the stand, to be cross-examined by Mr Simon Hugefee Q.C.)

Hugefee: Mr Sponge, I put it to you...

Mr Sponge: I'd rather you didn't!

(Laughter in public gallery)

Hugefee: I am obliged to you. Mr Sponge, Sir Spangle has shown you nothing but kindness and generosity over the many years of your professional and, dare I say it, intimate personal association. I am thinking in particular of his gift to you on 17 October 1997, as a gesture of reconciliation following an altercation between the two of you in Madame Yo-Yo's Pink Pussycat nightclub in St Tropez, of a solid gold toilet seat, encrusted with rubies. Do you remember that occasion, Mr Sponge?

Sir Spangle *(interrupting)*: She can't remember a thing. The silly cow was always pissed, not to mention doped up to the eyeballs.

Justice Cocklecarrot: Will you please restrain your client, Sir Hartley?

Sponge: She'd like that!

Public Gallery: Oooh!

Mr Justice Cocklecarrot: Will someone please remind me what this case is about, and who these people are?

The case continues.

"Hang on… I'm receiving a text message"

The Santiago Telegraph

FRIDAY DECEMBER 15 2000

LAMONT AWARD SHAME

by Our Political Staff **DOMINGUEZ LAWTHON**

CHILEAN public opinion has been outraged by the news that British politician Norman Lamont has been honoured by General Pinochet.

"This is a disgrace," said a spokesman. "We may not like General Pinochet much, but his involvement with an internationally reviled figure like Norman Lamont brings shame to the entire Chilean nation."

He continued, "Lamont was responsible for the disappearance of millions of pounds during the so-called Black Wednesday. He was never brought to trial for his crimes and continued to live a life of luxury visiting Threshers for sherry and cigars and letting out his property to Miss Whiplash and her friends."

THRASHERS

Lady Thatcher, a prominent supporter of Norman Lamont, was however quick to defend him. "Norman is a very sick man and has been for years. He had no idea what he was doing in the nineties and it's unfair to blame him on account of something that happened a long time ago."

ITV – Friday 7.30pm

40 Years Of Coronation Street Celebrations

A NOSTALGIC look back at forty years of programmes celebrating Coronation Street anniversary celebrations, including an interview with the man who originally had the bright idea of wall-to-wall celebrations with a sprinkling of C-list celebrities, and a special programme that celebrates the fact they've squeezed a few extra ratings out of clapped-out old-fashioned soap opera.

That New Labour Rural White Paper In Full

"Saving England's Green And Pleasant Land"

(HM Stationery Office £75)

FOREWORD by the Rt. Hon. John Prescott, Deputy Prime Minister, Saviour of the Planet and Secretary of State For Everything

DON'T get me wrong. I've got nothing against the countryside. I saw it once out of the window of one of my Jags. And now I've got the chance to do something about it, after 18 years of Tory neglect and mismanagement. I've been all over the countryside, listening to people. But unfortunately I can't remember anything they said.

However, this Government is determined to save the country side for future generations by turning it into a town.

John Prescott

Should The Guardian Be Abolished?

Phil Paperfordays
Royal Staff

TODAY we dare to ask the most important question in the history of Britain. Is it time to abolish the Guardian? Surely this creaking out-moded Victorian institution has outlived its usefulness and has no place in a modern go-ahead Britain. Don't get us wrong. We have nothing against the Guardian. It provides amusement for many people and offers a sort of escapism for those whose lives are lacking meaning. And some actually enjoy the pomp and the spectacle – the traditional sight of Alan Rusbridger making pronouncements on the issues of the day or the lesser members of the Guardian family sounding off on subjects about which they know very little.

Fair enough. But let us be honest for a minute. It really does not *matter* what the Guardian says. It has no power and has become largely irrelevant in today's society.

And then there is the matter of the cost of the Guardian – a staggering 45p a day. There may be a case for supporting the editor as a sort of figurehead but one has to ask whether we should still be paying for all those minor hangers-on given grace and favour columns in the newspaper.

One does not want to name names, but if Princess Polly of Toynbee, Lord Hugo the Young and Dame Julie Bullshit were all thrown out tomorrow nobody would care in the slightest *(cont. on all pages for weeks on end)*.

"Any of you girls good at darning socks?"

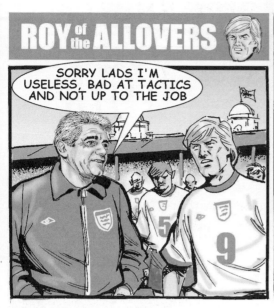

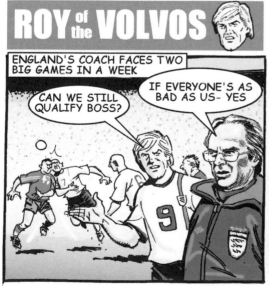

27

The Christmas Story Retold

From the Book of Common Rocky Horror Worship

1. And it came to pass in those days in the 4th year of the rule of Antoninus Blair that there went out a PR release to all the media that they should harken unto it.
2. And the message told of the glad tidings that the Madonna was to get married in Scotland.
3. And the wedding was to be held in the castle at Auchtermuchty, which is called Skibo.
4. And all the nation's journalists travelled together to Scotland but unfortunately there was not room in the Holiday Inn and some were forced to sleep in their cars.
5. And they were known as The Stupid Men from the East of London (Wapping).
6. And their names were McHackior, Bazbamingboye and Caspar Gerard from The Telegraph's Peterbore Column.
7. And they carried with them gifts of Gold, Frankincense and Murdoch.
8. And there were Shepherds in the fields watching Sky TV by night (pay as you view).
9. And behold they saw a star – and lo it was Madonna accompanied by her husband to be.
10. And his name was Guy which means "bloke" or "Diamond Geezer".
11. And Guy was taking the Madonna to the land of his birth to register their child with the authorities.
12. And the child's name was Rocco.
13. And so it was that the ancient prophecy was fulfilled. "Madonna will give birth to a boy child, the son of Guy, whose name shall be called Wonderful, Fantastic, Great, Cool, Wicked, Respect *(Cont. Chapter 94)*

(To be read in all churches at Christmas)

'Twas the night before Christmas, and all through the house
Not a creature was stirring except for the mouse...

THAT QUEEN'S SPEECH IN FULL

"MY GOVERNMENT will introduce a number of measures designed to persuade the punters to vote Labour next May. Don't worry if you don't like them much, because there won't be time to introduce any of them anyway. The really important one is the Abolition of the Foxhunting Bill. But don't get upset, because that won't get through in time either. Vote Labour and God Save Myself."

The Three Wise-after-the-event Men

CHRISTMAS FILMS
FAMILY ENTERTAINMENT

"The Railtrack Children" BBC1 Christmas Morning 7.30am

CHRISTMAS EVE SUNDAY

8.00pm (ITV)

"A Christmas Carol" (Made for TV, 1989). Gene Hackman stars as Lennie Scrooge, a Toronto businessman in this adaptation of the Dickens classic. McCaulay Caulkin is Tiny Tim and John Cleese pops up as the ghost of Hanukah Past. Songs by Burt Bacharach and Hal David (106 minutes)

BOXING DAY EVE MORNING

4.30am (C4)

"The Penguin With No Name" (1976). Comedy caper classic with Clint Eastwood teaming up with a penguin in an Antarctic circus rompt. Co-starring Sandra Locke (Mrs Eastwood) as good-time Innuit showgirl, Eskimo Nell. (207 minutes)

NEW YEAR'S AFTERNOON DAY

7.00pm (BBC1)

"Brains, Blood and Bollox" (1999). TV premiere of Guy Ritchie's acclaimed gangland classic set in Manchester's Moss side. Vinnie Jones stars as "Braindead Danny" who sets out to shoot everyone in Manchester through the mouth. Watch out for a superb bus chase sequence. (212 minutes)

NEW YEAR'S HOLIDAY SUNDAY EVE

3.30am (Sky Premiere)

The Muppets "War and Peace" (1994). Full-length feature of Tolstoy's classic with Kermit as Pierre Bozuhov, Fozzy Bear as Prince Andre and Miss Piggy as Natasha. Marlon Brando nearly steals the film as the Emperor Napoleon. Including the unforgettable song "I'm walking backwards from Moscow". (780 minutes)

"They Flew To Osaka" TCM (Black and white 1952). Cult Japanese re-make of the 1943 classic British war film "They Flew To Bruges". Directed by Kurosawa and relocated in the 14th century Samurai kingdom of Mitzubishi. The David Tomlinson role (Group Captain "Chalky" White) is taken by Tzumi Sushi. (10 hours) (That's enough films. Ed.)

KING ARRESTED

Everyone's gone to the police

The Wedding Of The Century

How They Are Related

Madonna	Guy Ritchie
Don Ciccone	Guy Fawkes
Don Corleone	Ritchie The Lionheart
Madonna Corleone	Sir Guy de Guisborne
Leonie Blair	Sir Guy the Gorilla
Tony Blair	Sir Lionel Ritchie
Madonna e Mobile	Lionel Bart
Madonna Kebab	Lionel Blair
MaDonna Summer	Tony Blair
Macaroni Ciccone	Sir Richie Benaud
Captain Corelli's Madonna	**Sir Cliff Ritchie**

(First Cousin Once Removed)

Lines On The Most Important Wedding In The History Of Scotland
by William Madonnagal

'Twas in the year 2000 of our Gracious Lord
That a woman got married whom the whole world adored.
As the popular American singer known as Madonna,
Vowed to Guy Ritchie that she would love, obey and honour (him),
Bells rang out across the glens
And the hotels filled up with her celebrity friends.
The lovely Gwyneth Paltrow and dashing Brad Pitt were there,
As was Sir Elton John and his amusing hair.
Stella McCartney designed the wedding dress
And a huge number of hacks flew into Inverness.
Great was the rejoicing amongst English papers
Who could fill their thin pages with these Highland capers,
"Madonna and Child and Guy Ritchie Too –
See page 1, 2, 3, 4, 5, 6, 7, 8, 9 and 52".
And as over Skibo Castle the sound of pipes soared
The entire nation got terrifically bored.
© Madonnagal 2000.

The Colin Cowdrey I Knew
by W.F. Deedes

IT WAS in 1892 that I firsht remember sheeing a young shchoolboy in short trousers coming out to bat for Shaint Cakesh in the annual Lords fixture againsht Fettesh. He went in at Number Shixsh, following E.L.B. Jackshon, brother of F.Sh. Jackshon, who of course later captained Yorkshire.

The young 12-year-old Cowdrey wash wholly unabashed by the occashion, and hit an unbeaten 5 not out before rain shtopped play.

Many yearsh later *(cont. p 94)*

HIGHGROVE, MONDAY

His Royal Highness the Prince of Wales will today fall off a horse. His condition will be stated to be "comfortable" after rumours that he had broken his neck proved to be untrue. He will be attended by the Mistress Royal, Mrs Camilla Parker-Biro, who will bring him newspapers in bed bearing the headlines "Ha! Ha! Ha! Serves you right, sire!".

PHUKET (THAILAND), TUESDAY

The Prince Andrew will continue with his royal duties of appearing on the front page of the tabloids. He will be attended by a number of topless lovelies, including Miss Brittany Ferries, Miss Titzi Glitzi and the Lady Victoria Starborgling (Country Life's Miss September 1998).

SANDRINGHAM, WEDNESDAY

The Princess Royal will attend the services of Matins, after which she will distribute the traditional New Year offensive remarks to members of the public. Mr and Mrs Sidney and Doris Saddoe will receive a "Get stuffed, you pathetic creeps. Get a life." Princess Anne will later apologise and claim to have been misquoted, her original words being "How kind of you to offer the Queen Mother such a delightful floral tribute. I shall give it to her personally. Now fuck off."

To The Editor Of Any Newspaper Who Is Desperate To Fill Up Space At New Year

Dear Sir,

I enclose my customary list of the most popular names for boys and girls in the past year.

BOYS	GIRLS
Harry	Nigella
Potter	Mariella
Becks	Posh
Wassup	Britney
Gerbil	Billie
Rocco	Nokia
Leo	Cherie
Railtrack	Madonna
Endeavour	Mo
Bob the Builder	Ann Widdecombe

Yours faithfully,

The Rev. Hewlett Packard,
The Old Photocopier,
Xerox, Hants.

OFFUCK
Watchdog
for Foul
Language

2001
NOW IT'S HERE
by Phil Space-Odyssey

IT IS exactly a hundred years since Kenneth C. Clarke wrote his chilling vision of the future, "2001 words by Friday, please". *(Surely "2001: A Space Odyssey"?)*

So how accurate were his predictions about the way we would live in the year 1984? *(That was Orwell. Ed.)*

Some of his forecasts have proved to be entirely correct.

● **Satellites ring the planet enabling us to communicate using global video conferencing facilities.**

● **Computers dominate every aspect of our lives and without** them human beings are helpless.

● **There is a large black monolith on the moon.**

But much of what he wrote has turned out to be well wide of the mark.

● **Man has not landed on Jupiter.**

● **No one drives around in Hovercars.**

● **There is no large black monolith on the moon.**

So, all in all, Arthur C's apocalyptic vision of the future is both disturbingly prescient and comfortingly wrong. He certainly never predicted that in this year alone his film would be repeated on 2001 channels 2001 times every week and *(cont. p. 2001)*

"Looks like the poison's working"

THE DAILY TELEGRAPH

Letter to the Editor

SIR – Those of us who sat through the so-called television adaptation of Auberon Waugh's Sword of Brideshead novels recently can only wonder at the ignorance of today's programme makers.

Did no one tell them that during the last war officers in the 49th Halfordeers ("The Black and Deckers") did *not* salute other ranks whilst wearing their caps even when, as in the evacuation of Crete, they had exchanged their normal headgear for makeshift handkerchiefs to keep off the sun?

Also, the idea that the hero Guy Hatchback would use the modern phrase "Good evening" when addressing Lady Starborgling, the second daughter of a Marquess would be laughable if it were not indicative of a wider malaise in the country as a whole.

Brigadier Sir Hector Keegan-Gussett,
The Old Pedantry,
St Evelyn, Somerset.

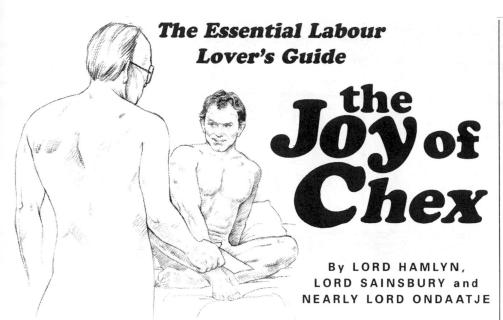

The Essential Labour Lover's Guide

the Joy of Chex

By LORD HAMLYN, LORD SAINSBURY and NEARLY LORD ONDAATJE

FOREPLAY

First you have to get into bed with your chosen partner, cosy up to them and slowly massage their egos. Then ask them if they would like to have chex.

THE CHEX ACT

Insert "the cash" into your partner's "account" as delicately and sensitively as possible. If it is done properly, this should give them a great deal of pleasure.

SAFE CHEX

Discretion is often an integral part of a healthy chex life. So don't tell anyone except your partner what you are up to. Privacy is all important, so take precautions!

VARIATIONS

It is worth experimenting with different sorts of chex and even different partners. You may get more satisfaction by swapping partners, say from Conservative to Labour, when they are no longer in government.

BONDAGE

With your partner tied to you, you can have fun exercising power with no responsibility! You may like to get your partner on their knees or bending over backwards to do what you say.

DRESSING UP

After chex you may want to dress up in funny clothes – like an ermine robe and a coronet. Don't be embarrassed just do it!

© Dr Alex Campbell.

2001
THE FACES TO WATCH

Who are they, the young movers and shakers whose faces are going to dominate Britain in the next year? From left to right:

■ **Jenny Jaycloth**, 22, avant-garde artist tipped to win the Turner Prize with her 24-hour video of paint drying.

■ **Nick Nerdie**, 23, dotcom wizard who launches his e-business web crawler "Flop" later this year. Already owes £47 million to the bank.

■ **Euan McEwan**, 23, star of BBC2's forthcoming adaptation of Gerry Adams' memoirs "Bomb of Honour".

■ **Rory Screamer**, 25, rising fashion designer who has just opened his own warehouse in up-and-coming Elephant and Castle. His Tweed and PVC 3-piece suits (with see-through crotch) are already being worn by about-towners such as Jonathan Ross and TV's Charles Moore.

■ **Fu Wotascorcha**, 19, Taiwanese-born clarinet prodigy who thrilled audiences at the Edinburgh Festival with her topless rendition of Mozart's Clarinet Concerto in B.

■ **Mike Fishwick**, 43, exciting new novelist (*That's enough Faces To Watch. Ed.*)

POLLY FILLER

Val D'Isère, Tuesday

CAN someone please, please explain the point of skiing? Wouldn't it be cheaper to climb into the freezer and throw fifty pound notes down the drain?

And this is supposed to be fun? I stupidly gave in when the useless Simon threatened to go off on his own, leaving yours truly in sole charge (apart from Ivanka obviously) of a furious toddler

who is still angry with Santa Claus because he got a Playstation 2 (£285) instead of a Bob The Builder soft toy. Talk about ungrateful!

Anyway, the next thing I know we're all four of us (Ivanka with the luggage) queuing up at Gatwick looking like Michelin Men in day-glo skiwear that would make even Kate Moss look like Vanessa Feltz!

And what a miserable five star chalet awaited us, with some dim blonde girl trying to cook cordon bleu cuisine and ruining the most simple dishes by flirting with Simon. (*Don't you mean "putting too much cream in the Pave de Boeuf en Blue D'Auvergne"? Ed.*)

Luckily, she left in tears after I complained to the Rep and she was replaced by a hunky Australian called Guy who Simon rather pathetically allowed to make him feel inadequate and jealous. Men! Really! Things went downhill(!) after that! Someone had failed to tell me that skiing means going up a mountain! In winter?!

OK, the scenery is quite nice in a chocolate boxy sort of way, but if the company didn't want me

to get vertigo, the stupid girl at the caisse shouldn't have sold me a lift pass.

When they finally stopped all the lifts and prised me out of the bubble car I said it was a disgrace and I was never going to ski again. Everyone seemed to think this was a good idea and clapped wildly.

MEANWHILE, Charlie cried all day in the snow-crèche and the stupid French girls tried to talk to him in French – it must have been *obvious* he was English!

No wonder he bit the little girl sitting beside him at lunch. They should have known that Charlie only eats fish fingers for lunch – with peanut butter on them. Have they no experience of toddlers at all?

What a disaster! So, if anyone tells you they've had fun ski-ing, remember – they are not only mad, but they are lying as well. *I* know. I've been there, done that and got the t-bar.

© Polly Filler

INTERNET SALE TWINS' FIRST WORD

Money!

"Ah, the pitter patter of tiny feet"

THE SCANDAL OF BABIES FOR SALE

by Our Adoption Staff **Will Foster**

A BRITISH man who has successfully purchased a baby was at the centre of an ethical storm last night amidst calls for an end to "this appalling trade".

The man, a Mr Stuart Wheeler, who is the chief executive of a betting company, simply paid £5 million and purchased little William Hague.

"I've always wanted a politician of my own," said Mr Wheeler, "and now I have one I am delighted. No one is going to take him away from me."

There was, however, a furious reaction from a Mr Michael Ashcroft who was under the impression that *he* had bought little William for £1 million when he was just "a foetus".

"I was looking after William and providing a secure environment in which he could grow up. Then along comes someone else and offers more money. It's a disgrace."

DUMMY

Moral campaigners are worried that Britain is following the example of the United States and allowing baby-faced politicians to be bought for cash.

"It's obscene," said a spokesman. "Only last month there was a scramble over who would own little Tony and now we have the unseemly spectacle of baby William being sold to the highest bidder.

"What about unwanted babies like little Charles Kennedy who sadly *(cont'd. p. 94)*

JANET AND JOHN

Janet is best friends with Elton John. They love to play. See Janet play. See Elton John play.

Elton John loves flowers. "Look at all my lovely flowers, Janet," he says. "What a lot of fahkin' flowers," says Janet. "Look at all the fahkin' flowers, children."

"I've got lots of shirts too," says Elton John. "Millions of fahkin' shirts," says Janet. "That's fahkin' fantastic."

Janet likes to play at newspapers. "You can be in my newspaper," she tells Elton John. See! Elton John is in Janet's newspaper on page three. And on page five. And on page six. And in the Diary. And in the magazine.

"We are going on holiday," says Elton John. "Come to Hawaii with me on the aeroplane."

See Janet go to Hawaii on the aeroplane with Elton John. Or is it Nice this week, or New York?

See! The hacks at the *Indie on Sunday* do not go on the aeroplane. They stay behind in Docklands.

World of Boxing

STANDING OVATION FOR 'GREATEST-EVER' CHAMPION

by Our Man At The Ringside **Harrods Carpenter**

HE WAS the greatest. That was the unanimous verdict of thousands of celebrities who gathered at the Dorchester Hotel yesterday to honour Mohamed Ali Fayed, former World Heavyweight Liar and Champion Crook Of All Time.

"I am the fuggin' greatest!" the champion told his audience, delighting them with endless repetition of his celebrated catchphrase, "Fug like a butterfly, fug like a bee".

He was then led away by his manager Mr Clifford, who said "Mohamed has got Parkinson's Disease – he wants to be on the show, and I think I can fix it for him."

From The Great Bunker In The Sky

Achtung!

So, Mr Blair, you thought that, just because I am dead, you had heard the last of me and my all-conquering Referendum Party.

(Strokes ghost of white cat in sinister fashion)

Well, I have news for you, Double-O Blair. My top agent (codename Lady Annabel Fishpaste) is still very much alive and, how you say, kicking, nicht war?

And this time she is armed with a deadly secret weapon. Five hundred thousand highly-trained English pounds, which are targeted to wipe out the whole of Europe!

With one flick of a switch, Mr Blair, you and your friends will all go up in a puff of smoke!

I am disappointed in you, Mr Blair. I thought maybe we could do business together.

But I see now you are just another ordinary, dull, little politician like all the others.

Goodbye, Mr Bond!

Issued on behalf of the late Referendum Party (aka SMERSH) by Lady Evita Goldfish, Richmond Park, Planet Earth.

If you would like to join the great crusade to waste the money of the late Sir James Goldfinger, please apply at once for psychiatric help. Or visit our website on www.jampaste.dotty.con

"I'm rather worried about levels of stress in the office"

St Cakes

Transsexual Term begins today. There are 397 girls in the school who used to be boys. Miss C.J.P. Gender-Bender (Hormones) is Head Boy. Miss D.J. Surgical-Procedure (Clinics) is Captain of Lacrosse (formerly Rugby). The Cross(Dress) Country Run will be held on March 7th. The Jan-Morris-Dancing Society will perform on April 3rd (Founderess Day). The Headmaster, Mr R.J. Kipling, wishes to be known from now on as Mrs Dorothy Prendergast. Exeats will be to Sweden on April 11th.

St Cakes is a leading independent public school in the Midlands (No. 1,798 in the National League Tables).

CHARLOTTE CHURCH AT HARRODS

Fancy a quick fugue?

BOYS IN BLUE SUFFER AFTER RECENT DAMNING CRITICISM

by Our Police Staff **Sir Paul Flavoured-Condon**

THE CONSERVATIVES are losing recruits after they were branded "institutionally useless" in a report by a senior Judge.

"Morale is rock bottom," said a spokesman. "Recruitment is at an all-time low and Tories are leaving the force in their thousands.

"They have lost the support of the ethnic communities," he continued, "even in areas such as Tunbridge Wells."

On a typical estate in Surrey (Sir Reginald Frobisher's Clapton Hall, 978 acres) where there used to be Tories in abundance, there is now only one Tory within 100 miles.

"You can go for days," said 87 year old Lady Victoria Hooray, "without seeing a single Tory with their reassuring uniform of tweed jackets, corduroy trousers and shooting sticks. Nowadays they are all in their cars or sitting in offices staring at computer screens.

"No wonder," she said, "people like me are afraid to go out at night."

The Mail Says Ban This Revolting Picture

OPIUM
the fragrance from
YVES SAINT LAURENT

ON OTHER PAGES: Other pictures which are too revolting to show.

I'm here for two terms

BIRT MAN TO GET TOP OPERA JOB

by Our Opera Staff **Tagliatelle Verdi**

THE WORLD of opera was rocked to its foundations last night when it was announced that a senior BBC figure is to be the new supremo of the Royal Opera House, Covent Garden.

He is Mr Tony Hall, 54, former head of the BBC's prestigious news department, who is best known for wearing a suit and a pair of glasses.

Shock

Mr Hall immediately an-nounced his shock 405-point plan for "streamlining and modernising" Covent Garden. These include:

● moving the opera house to White City to make it "more efficient and user friendly"

● to move it back to Covent Garden five years later, after realising that no one wanted to go to White City

● moving all opera perform-ances to a "10 o'clock at night slot", to attract a larger audience

● moving them all back again to

7 o'clock after realising that no one was watching

● creating an "internal market" where the singers have to pay for their costumes, and the orchestra hires the score from the Opera House

● abolishing the "internal market" when it is realised that it is losing money

● "rolling opera" available in the foyer 24 hours a day, so that audiences can access opera at all times.

Those New Tony Hall Opera Productions In Full

Mozart's The Magic Roundabout

Mozart's Don G. Armani

Wagner The Ring Nick Ross

Monteverdi The Coronation Street of Poppen

Monteverdi's Flying Circus (repeat)

Bizet Carmen In Suits

(That's enough operas. Ed.)

My Secret Shame

By Charles Spencer

For years I had been trying to hide my guilty secret from my friends, my family and myself.

But then one night my wife discovered me slumped over a word processor and I had to face the truth.

Yes, I write for the Daily Telegraph.

But now I am completely cured and that is why, as proof, I have written a huge piece about my problem in the Daily Telegraph.

There was no point in denying it any longer. What had started with just a couple of pieces had become a full-blown career.

Blotto Paper

My friends thought I was just an amiable middle-aged drunk who fell asleep underneath rhododendron bushes. But, in reality, I was hiding from them the fact that I was seeking every opportunity to nip into Canary Wharf and get utterly published.

Luckily, I have now received help from Telegraph Anonymous, a support group for those who can't resist "putting a few pieces away". I have at last recognised that I have a problem and that my behaviour over the last few years has been a disgrace. I look back at some of my articles and cringe with embarrassment.

Charles Boozer's Top Plays of 2000

● Four Gentlemen Of Verona

● Twelve Characters In Search Of A Drink

● The Long, The Short And The Tall Glass Please Barman

● The Blue Room Appears To Be Going Round

● Anything At The Under The Bush Theatre, Hampstead

(That's enough plays. Ed.)

DEPLETED URANIUM 'A TRIUMPH' says Minister

by Our Defence Staff
Michele Shock

GEOFF HOON, the Secretary of State for Defence, last night defended the use of depleted uranium on the battlefield.

"For years, British weapons have been criticised for not working. Guns have jammed, tanks have malfunctioned and bombs have missed their targets.

"Now, at last, we have a weapon that actually kills people. Unfortunately, it is our own troops and civilians on the other side. Still, it's a start."

Geoff Hoohee is 57 GigaHertz.

The Little Red Ken Goes To New York

ONE day little Red Ken went to New York. "I am going off to see the Mayor," he said. And on the way, Ken noticed that all the streets were as clean as a whistle, everyone was happy and smiling, there were no muggers and all the subway trams ran on time. "Goodness me," cried the little Red Ken, as he looked up at all the exciting tall buildings. "Wouldn't it be lovely if London was like this?" "And so it can be," said a genial figure, who turned out to be the Mayor himself. "I am Mayor Stringemup," he told the little Red Ken, "how about you and your little pet newt coming for a ride with me in this elevator?"

And so they went up to the 112th floor, where they looked out at Mayor Stringemup's city. And the Mayor told the Red Ken the secret of how it was done. " When people are naughty," he said, "we bring them up here and throw them off. I call it zero-tolerance."

And the little Red Ken said, "What a good idea! I must write about this in the Guardian when I go home."

NEXT WEEK: The little Red Ken tries to starve all the Trafalgar Square pigeons to death.

NEWS IN BRIEF

Victoria's 100th Anniversary Commemorated

ALL of Britain's tabloids this week commemorated the anniversary of the 100th front page story featuring Victoria Beckham.

"It's incredible to think there was a time when Victoria and her consort David didn't totally dominate the minds of our editors," said one delighted hack.

"Truly the Sun will never set on Victoria's empire," he added, "and neither will the Mirror, the Star, the Express or the Mail."

(Reuters)

'Soft Touch' Claim

THERE were claims today that the Daily Mail was a soft touch for asylum seekers' stories.

"More asylum seeker articles have ended up there than at any other newspaper," said one gypsy. "A lot of these articles should have been rejected out of hand and sent packing, but lax editorial controls have allowed them to slip through the net.

"The question has to be asked, why? It's almost as if they're being encouraged to turn up here."

"It's true that over the past year there's been a ten-fold increase in badly researched articles and woefully written comment pieces," said concerned Daily Mail readers. "Frankly, we've been overwhelmed by them, and still they keep coming."

(Reuters)

May I have this dunce?

Slow, slow, slow, slow, slow

Young George W. Bush

"Of course, the so-called environmentalists would have us believe that it's wrong to chop down trees"

■ TV Highlights

Rebel Viewers
BBC1 Sunday

STIRRING story of a popular revolt against the hated British Broadcasting Corporation who were occupying the Sunday evening schedules with dreary historical Irish drama.

Will the people put up with it? Or will they rise up en masse from their armchairs and turn over to watch "It'll be Alright on the Night 7" with Dennis Norden?

HOW DARE I RESIGN?

by Peter Mandelson

THERE has been a terrible miscarriage of justice, and I can keep silent no longer.

My loyalty to Tony Blair is second to none. But in this case I have to speak out.

He should never have accepted my resignation when I offered it to him.

He should have known that I was demoralised after days of remorseless hounding by the media, baying for blood.

Tony should never have summoned me to Downing Street, to face a kangaroo court made up of himself and his friend Mr Campbell.

I was not allowed to plead my case, nor even to have my solicitor present. What justice is there in that, I ask?

I was grilled relentlessly for five minutes, and asked all sorts of impossible questions designed to catch me out, like "Did you make that call to Mike O'Brien, Peter, or not?"

Honestly, how can anyone be expected to remember whether they made a particular telephone call two years ago?

The two of them were just like the Gestapo. They fired question after question at me, as though I was some sort of criminal.

"Look, Peter, Jack says you made the call. So does Mike. Can you remember whether you did or not?"

No wonder that after a few minutes of this I was totally dazed and confused.

I couldn't believe it! After all,

these were meant to be my friends!

Yet here they were, beating a confession out of me like something out of Stalin's Russia!

"Ok," I said finally, "I give in. I confess. I did it! I'll resign, whatever you want. Only just stop asking me about the 'phone call."

Then Alastair handed me a sheet of paper. "Here is your confession," he said. "Go out and read it to the waiting journalists."

Like a fool, I agreed. I went out and did exactly as he said, as if I was a sleepwalker.

That is what brain-washing is all about.

And then, as if that was not enough, the next morning I was forced to read all these terrible headlines in the newspapers, making out that I was mad and had been sacked after having a nervous breakdown.

So much for loyalty, Alastair! So much for friendship, Tony!

If anyone is mad, it is you two. Particularly Alastair. I always warned you, Tony, not to trust him. And I was right. I knew that sooner or later he would let you down. But you wouldn't listen.

And I can tell you this. You will live to regret it. I am not a vindictive man. All I want is to clear my name.

I have no desire to betray all the government's secrets just before an election. And, of course, I would never dream of selling my memoirs to Mr Murdoch for £1 million, even though he has offered me this sum.

I know only too well what terrible damage this could inflict on the Project, if certain things were to come out about certain people in the last few weeks of what could be a very close election, now that your popularity has collapsed in the wake of my unforgiveable resignation.

All I want is for the record to be put straight over the supposed telephone call to Mr O'Brien. The essential facts are:

1. It was all a long time ago.

2. I cannot remember whether I remember the call or not.

3. I certainly cannot be expected to answer any questions now that the whole affair is the subject of a comprehensive enquiry by Sir Wally Whitewash QC.

4. My resignation is thus rescinded and I should be given back my job as Foreign Secretary and Deputy-Prime Minister immediately.

It is still possible, I hope, for all this to be sorted out in a civilised and grown-up way.

Rt. Hon. P. Mandelson
P.C. M.P.

PS. I hate you all.

J'ACCUSE

by Top Author Emile Zola Harris

THIS government is responsible for the most disgusting act of treachery and conspiracy in the sordid annals of world politics. My friend, Captain Gayfuss, has become the innocent victim of a sinister plot without parallel in human *(cont. p. 94)*

■ Film Choice

Peter's Friendless

CLASSIC English comedy where a group of old friends gather together in a large house in Downing Street and put the boot into Peter Mandelson. Heavily indebted to the *Big Chill* but still entertaining. Don't miss the climax where Peter reveals that he is gay and dying to get his own back. Starring Kenneth Branagh as Alastair Campbell, Tony Slattery as Peter Mandelson and Hugh Laurie as Tony Blair.

GLENDA SLAGG

Fleet Street's Gal In The Front Line!!?!

Women in the front line!?!?! Don't make me laugh!!! OK, so us gals can do anything men can do – and do it better!?!?! But why should we join in and do their dirty work for them??! If they want to kill each other and blow each other's brains out, that's fine – but don't ask me to come a-lootin' and a-shootin'!?!? OK????? Atten-shun!!!

Have you heard the latest?!?! The bumbling brass hats in the War Office are trying to stop us gals joining in World War Three!! We've got as much right to be there as anyone else?!!? What are you scared of, Mr Commander-in-Chief?!?!? Do you think we might run off with the Sergeant at the first opportunity?!?!? You must be B-Army!!?! Geddit?!?! At Ease!!?!

Those Mitford Girls – arenchasickofthem? Debbo, Nancy and the other one!?!? Everywhere you look there they are on the telly, in the papers, in my column?!?!? A load of posh girls sitting around a-robbin' and a-snobbin' with all the celebs of years gone by !?! So

they met Adolf Hitler??! Who didn't!!?! Give us a break, Auntie Beeb, or we'll give them a Missford!?!? Geddit??!?!!

Hoorah for the Mitford Girls!?! Those dare-devil debs of yesteryear who paved the way for the liberated lasses of today!?!? I call them the "It-ford Girls" (Geddit?!?!) Period hats off to Binty, Bunty, Chico, Harpo and Adolf!?!?! And cheers too to the good old Auntie Beeb for giving us another giant dollop of these funky flappers of a bygone age!!?!

Here they are – Glenda's Valentine Cards (Geddit?!?!!)

Francis Maude MP – He wants a gay Prime Minister!! Each to his own, Maudie – I prefer them straight!?!?!

Keith Vaz – OK, so he's fat, Indian and bent – that's the way I like them!!?!

Robert Harris – I could do with a spicy thriller to take to bed at night – though why he likes Mandy is a bit of an Enigma!?!! (Geddit??!?!)

Byeeeeeee!!!!!!!!!

"It's too late, Bob, I've found someone else"

PEACE PROCESS FALTERS – ADAMS FLIES IN

by Our Northern Ireland Staff **Martin McGunless**

FEARS were growing in Westminster last night that the fragile peace in the Labour Party would be destroyed with the departure of the Northern Ireland Secretary, Peter Mandelson.

Talks between Mandelson and government spokesman Alastair Campbell have broken down and there is no communication whatsoever between the two camps.

Mr Mandelson is refusing to decommission his lawyers and Mr Campbell has broken the ceasefire by firing off a couple of cheap shots about Peter being "semi-deranged".

Londonderry Irvine

Peacemaker Gerry Adams has now flown in to London in an attempt to stop the fighting escalating into a full-blown civil war.

"I am here to help," he laughed. "The two sides have got to sit down at the table and negotiate a lasting peace. Ha ha ha ha ha ha."

Friends of Mr Mandelson said nothing because there aren't any.

"I'm getting in touch with my feminine side!"

Letters to the Editor

Women On The Front Line

SIR – As one with his fair share of experience of combat, I can testify that the presence of women on the battlefield is entirely inappropriate.

The loss of morale that would be occasioned by the death or injury of a female comrade-in-arms would inevitably lead to desertion on a huge scale – as indeed happened at the Battle of Monopylae (391 BC) when the invading Phoenicians were put to flight following the death of Princess Greia of Germania who had disguised herself as a man, if the historian Strepsilides is to be believed.
Brigadier P.J.D. Farqharson-Trubshaw, The Old Brothel, Sherborne, Dorset.

SIR – I fail to understand what all the fuss is about. If women can sail single-handedly round the globe, become prime minister of Britain and win the Women's Singles at Wimbledon, why on earth should they not be given the right to take their place alongside their male comrades in the war cemeteries of the world?
Col. J.A. Frobisher (Mrs), The Old Battleaxe, Battle, Sussex.

SIR – In the 1939-45 war, as we read in Count Nikolai Tolstoy's epic work *Believe It Or Not*, entire divisions of the Red Army were made up of women, including all the tank crews who fought in the terrible battle of Michaelgrad. These women lived for months at a time on a diet of nothing but diesel oil and frozen bootleather, but succeeded in defeating a German army of more than a million crack SS troops under the command of Field Marshal "Hitler" Hastings.
Sir John Trumper-Smythe (Defence Editor, Daily Telegraph 1875-1938), The Old Bunker, St. Alingrad, Wilts.

SIR – Why should women want to fight in men's wars anyway? Why not let men kill each other, as they have done since time began, instead of offering ourselves as targets for their patriarchal, phallo-centric killing fields?
Not yours (or any other man's),
Deirdre Spart, Department of Non-Military History and Post-Feminist Studies, University of Womanchester (formerly Cheadle Hulme Polytechnic).

SIR – It is all very well to want to put women in the front line, but where are they going to pin medals on them?
Mike Giggler, via e-mail.

Delhi Telegraph

Friday, February 9, 2001

MILLIONS OF BELIEVERS GATHER FOR WORLD'S BIGGEST EVER HINDUJA FESTIVAL

by Our Man In The River Thames ANDREW MARRHARAJAH

THE SALLY JOCKSTRAP INTERVIEW

Sven Goran-Eriksson

IT HAS been billed as the biggest gathering of devotees of the goddess Muni the world has ever seen.

From all over Britain they have come, to purify themselves by washing away their debts in the holy river of Muni.

Devout followers of Hinduja believe that they can achieve the mystical state of *veryishi* by making contact with the three Hinduja deities, Gotalot, Kashna and Bakhanda.

ALMS DEALERS

I spoke to a typical group of Hinduja-ists, all of whom happened to be members of the British parliament.

"The coming of Hinduja into our lives has been the most wonderful blessing," said one elderly grocer who had travelled all the way from Salisbury to bathe in the holy money.

"I have long believed in the healing properties of Hinduja-ism," said the grocer with a smile, "and now I am laughing all the way to the banks of the Ganges."

VAZ WASHES WHITER

But it is not only to the old that

Hinduja-ism appeals. A new generation of believers have joined the pilgrimage, led by their guru Keith Vaz.

"As easily the most important Asian person in Britain today," he said, "I give my unequivocal support to this festival."

KUM MOOLAH

With such huge numbers of people queuing up to share in "the blessings of Hinduja", it is not surprising that there are

occasional casualties.

All Britain has been shocked by the story of one young mystic, Gahatma Mandi, who was paying homage to the Hindujas when he slipped, and was swept away by the muddy waters, never to be heard of again.

Said his friend Robert Hari Krishna, "It is a terrible tragedy. He did not jump, he was pushed."

Another young worshipper, William Hague, on the banks of the Natwest *(cont)*

I TRAVELLED to Aintree, the Mecca of Britain's golfers, to meet the man who is going to put English cricket back on the map.

Sally: Sven, a good result for your team on Saturday against the Welsh. How do you rate your chances of winning back the Davis Cup?

Sven: I think drinking alcohol always affects a player's ability to kick the ball in a negative fashion.

Sally: Yes, but we're here to talk about boxing, Sven. Surely it's time for Michael Schumacher to hang up his boots?

Sven: It is time to bring in young players who show potential talent for kicking the ball in an intelligent fashion.

Sally: Does that mean you're going to leave out Frankie Dettori?

Sven: English house prices are very expensive for sure. Such a lot of money for tiny house – not even room to swing a mouse! You must be crazy, no?

© *All newspapers.*

EMBARRASSING HINDUJA PHOTO

How embarrassing!

I know. This isn't going to do our reputation any good

VOICE OF The Mirror

THE campaign against Keith Vaz is an utter disgrace and smacks of the most shameless racism on the part of the Tories and their tame toadies in the press.

What is his alleged offence? That he might have used his position to line his pockets?

So what? Who hasn't? That's what we all do here. It's certainly not something you should lose your job over.

Well done, Vazzer! You're an example to us all.

© *Piers Moron, the most prominent member of Britain's journalistic community.*

CRIME FIGURES ARE UP OR DOWN
Knacker Spells It Out

by Our Crime Staff **Nicked Ross** and **Sue Crook**

AT A major press conference attended by Home Secretary Jack Straw, Inspector "Knacker of the Yard" Knacker yesterday announced that crime figures were up or down, according to which way you hold the graph.

Holding it one way up, Britain's top policeman pointed to a huge fall in last year's crime figures, showing what a superb job he and his colleagues had done.

He then turned the graph upside down, to show an alarming increase in crime, which demonstrated the vital need for billions more pounds to be spent on hiring millions more police officers.

P.C. World

At this point, Mr Straw intervened to congratulate Inspector Knacker on his "superb achievement" in getting crime both up and down at the same time.

"This government," he said, "is committed to getting everything up and down. Waiting lists are up, operations are down. Class sizes are up, standards are down. Labour are up, the Tories are down. It all makes sense whichever way you look at it."

euritannia (rebranded)

THE BOOK OF SHARON

1. And it came to pass, in the days of the intifada, that the children of Israel grew weary of the process called peace.

2. And they said amongst themselves, who is this man Bar-ak, son of E-hud, whom we have appointed to rule over us?

3. For he hath promised us a land flowing with milk and money, where the children of Israel would live in peace with the Arab-ites and the Araf-ites, even as the cocatrice lieth down with the porcupine.

4. But, lo, he delivereth it not.

5. For, verily, they said, the Arab-ites and the Araf-ites rise up in the streets of Gaza and in the hills of Hebron, and cast their stones upon us, crying "Go home, o ye children of Israel, even to A-mer-ica and R-ussia from whence ye came."

6. And the children of Is-rael waxed exceeding wroth at the thought of the Ara-bites getting away with it.

7. And there was dwelling in the land, an elder of the people whose name was Shar-on, which is to say the terminator.

8. And Shar-on was old and his skin was shrivelled, even as the walnut in the grove of Gil-ead that hath been dried in the heat of the noon-day sun.

9. And the children of Israel came unto Shar-on privily, and saith unto him "This Bar-ak is no bloody good."

10. And Shar-on saith unto them, "Thou hast spoken truly. For he preacheth peace and the result is war."

11. "I, on the other hand," saith Shar-on, son of Likud, "am a man who preacheth war which will bring you peace."

12. "For I say unto you that the only good Araf-ite is an dead Araf-ite."

13. And the children of Israel rose up and with one voice they called him "Cabba", which is to say, one who driveth an cab and speaketh the truth through a glass partition darkly.

14. And they said, "Let Shar-on rule over us." And so it came to pass, and Bar-ak was cast out, even into outer darkness (until he was asked back to join the Cabinet).

15. And the children of Israel rejoiced mightily. And they sang and danced and blew tributes to Sharon, even on the horns of their chariots.

16. And they said unto themselves: "Now, truly, we shall have peace. For the Araf-ites and the Hamas-ites will be too terrified of Shar-on to cause any more trouble."

17. But things did not come to pass in this wise.

18. For everything turneth into the shape of an pear, even the pear that groweth on the avocado tree that groweth in ther groves of Car-mel (buy one, get one free).

19. For the Araf-ites and the Hezboll-ites had learned a thing or two about smiting from the Children of Israel and had decided that this time they would get their smiting in first.

20. And so they did, even an hundredfold.

21. And there was much wailing and gnashing of teeth amongst the Children of Israel, who said unto one another: "This wasn't the idea at all. For it is meant to be the other way round."

22. And Shar-on said: "It will be. Just you wait."

23. And so it continueth, even unto the Day of Judgement.

(To be continued)

Lookalikes

Frankenstein   **Martin Amis**

Sir,

Don't you think there is an uncanny resemblance between Frankenstein's monster and the embalmed-looking Martin Amis, author of 'Dead Babies'?

How often does he need to plug his fingers in the alternating current? I think we should be told.

Yours truly,
ROGER LEWIS,
Bromyard, Herefordshire.

Brenda   **Tubbs**

Sir,

An informally attired Brenda bears a striking resemblance to Tubbs from BBC2's League of Gentlemen. A local monarch for local people, perhaps?

Yours (with dark and brooding humour),
JACQUELINE PERKS & MARK SMITH,
Buckingham.

Jack   **Liz**

Sir,

Have any of your readers noticed the amazing resemblance of Liz Dawn (ubiquitous "Corrie" actress) to Jack Nicholson as the "Joker" in "Batman"?

Maybe they are related. I think we should be told.

Yours faithfully,
E. MOORE (MRS),
Formby, Merseyside.

Alfred E. Neumann   **George W. Bush**

Sir,

Have any of your readers noticed the uncanny similarity between the comic character George "Dubya" Bush and Alfred "Eeeee" Neumann, the internationally respected face 0f MAD magazine?

DONALD DYER,
Florida, USA.

Jagger   **Grinch**

Sir,

Did the Grinch steal Christmas? Or has he been falsely accused? I think we should be told.

Yours faithfully,
MATT O'DONNELL,
Reading, Berks.

Milosevic   **Burchill**

Sir,

I wonder if any of your readers have noticed the peculiar physical similarity between the harshly-spoken Julie Burchill with the teflon septum, quondam News of the World columnist and "Queen of the Groucho Club"; and Marija Milosevic, the style-queen of Serbia and daughter of the Stalinist war-criminal Slobodan Milosevic.

Could they, by any chance, be related?

Yours,
EDNA WELTHORPE (MRS),
Oxford.

Glenconner   **Meldrew**

Sir,

Have any of your readers noticed the amazing resemblance between the bad-tempered pensioner Lord Glenconner and the archetypal English gentleman Victor Meldrew?

Are they by any chance related?

Yours,
SIR ARTHUR QUILLER-COUCHPOTATO

London N6.

Tito   **Dr Evil**

Sir,

Has anyone else noticed the uncanny resemblance between Dennis Tito, the bald, crazy-eyed multi-millionaire scientist recently orbiting the Earth in a dangerous space station and Dr Evil, Austin Powers' deadly adversary?

Yours, with my Mojo intact,
DAI HICKS,
Via e-mail.

Wheen   **Duncan Smith**

Sir,

The Tory Party crashes from one disaster to another. Do they not realise the dangers of moving to the left in their current search for a leader? Iain Duncan Smith is shurely a very poor attempt to enter Grauniad journo and Karl Marx biographer Francis Wheen into the leadership election race.

Photographic evidence of this withheld, name and address willingly supplied.

Yours faithfully,
E. BENNET,
London E14.

Carpenter   **Gadaffy**

Sir,
    Have you noticed the strange resemblance between Colonel Gadaffy Duck and the Carpenter from "Alice in Wonderland"?
    I wonder if their crocodile tears might be genetically related?
        Yours oysterly,
        LOUIS HELLMAN,
London W3.

Williams   **Redwood**

Sir,
    Shame they never got round to making "Carry On Conservative". A bit late now. I suppose, if they did, John Redwood could certainly take Kenneth Williams' role.
        Yours etc,
        ENA B. RUSHTON,

London W1.

JUST FANCY THAT!

"Editor's Note: Would readers please stop sending in the accompanying photographs highlighting the complete lack of resemblance between the e-fit released by police involved in the Jill Dando inquiry and the prime minister's press secretary, Alastair Campbell."
    — Eye 976, 14 May 1999

"The prime minister's press secretary, Alastair Campbell, was interviewed by detectives investigating the murder of Jill Dando, the television presenter."
    — Sunday Times front-page story,
        12 November 2000

Not Related

Kray Brothers   **Barclay Brothers**

Sir,
    Lookalike or what!
        Yours,
        JO BIRCH,
Petie Moie, Sark.

Troll   **Blair**

Sir,
    There appears to be a strong resemblance between the lifeless, plastic, humour-inducing figure above, and the favourite children's toy. The world should be told!
        Yours,
        STEVEN ALGIERI,
Hayling Island, Hants.

Duchess   **Geri**

Sir,
    Has the singing of former Spice Girl Geri Halliwell improved so much that she can now get a place in the back row of the Bach Choir, or has the Duchess of Kent had one too many vitamin injections? I think we should be told.
        Yours,
        MATTHEW RYE,
Leighton Buzzard, Beds.

Neanderthal Man   **Chris Smith**

Sir,
    So now we know: they **are** related.
        Yours faithfully,
        GARETH REEVES,

Durham.

Archer   **Robinson**

Sir,
    I've recently noticed the similarity between these two justice-seekers. Are they egotistically related?
        Yours,
        PETER BRADLEY,
Kettering, Northants

Jackson   **Ape**

Sir,
    Does anybody else see a similarity between Helena Bonham-Carter's ape character from the remake of The Planet of the Apes and the remade and remodelled Michael Jackson?
        DR CHARLES VAUGHAN-JONES,
Montgomery, Powys.

Coin   **Maggie**

Sir,
    Found a rather familiar face in an 1892 publication "Atlas de Monnaies Gauloises" by Henri De La Tour.
    The coin is from Brittany in the First Century BC. Is reincarnation a likely prospect? I think we should be told.
        Yours sincerely,
        IMOGEN WELLINGTON,
Dept of Archaeology, University of Durham.

Shrek   **Danny**

Sir,
    Has anyone else noticed the uncanny similarity between the two-dimensional computer-generated film character Shrek, and Danny from the two-dimensional Popstars-generated band, Hear'say?
        A. BROWN,
Via e-mail.

BLAIR ANNOUNCES INQUIRY INTO EVERYTHING

by Our Political Staff **Michael Whitewash** and **Simon Hogwash**

THE Prime Minister yesterday silenced his critics by setting up an official inquiry into "absolutely everything".

The inquiry will be headed by one of the country's leading lawyers, a man of whom nobody had heard until today.

Friends describe him as "intensely able, a real high-flyer, with a First Class rail ticket and striped trousers".

SHOCK

The terms of the inquiry are to include:

- the breakdown of Britain's transport system
- the collapse of the National Health Service
- the crisis in Britain's schools
- the explosion in the prison population
- asylum seekers
- the spread of HIV
- the need to cull badgers, pigeons, foxes, etc
- global warming
- the Hinduja brothers' passport application
- the argument between Miss Zara Phillips and her boyfriend outside a pub.

The fact that all these matters are to be subject to the judicial inquiry means that no one is allowed to comment on any of them until the inquiry has delivered its verdict just after the election.

When the Conservatives complained that this would have the effect of silencing all political debate for the foreseeable future, Mr Blair announced that this would be the subject of a further inquiry, to report in the year 2020, and that therefore he could not possibly comment.

OXFORD UNIVERSITY

English Language And Literature

Finals

(Set by Professor John Bayley)

1. Imagine that you are an elderly don formerly married to a famous novelist but now short of a bob or two. Describe, in your own words, a pathetic sexual fantasy in which various women get into bed with you.

2. Analyse the relationship between fact and fiction in English Literature, with special reference to *Keeping It Up* by J. Bayley (2001).

3. "The Telegraph has really wasted its money this time." Discuss.

4. Is Alzheimer's contagious?

Time allowed: ten minutes.
Send completed papers to Charles Moore, Editor, The Bayley Telegraph, Canary Wharf, enclosing a large invoice.

DYKE SAYS BBC 'HIDEOUSLY BAD'

by Our Media Staff **Michael White**

IN A SHOCK interview last night the director-general of the BBC, Mr Greg Dyke, admitted that the BBC was "institutionally rotten".

He told journalists: "I am shocked to find that every time I turn on the TV I see the face of someone who is no good."

He continued: "98% of our staff are hideously bad — including myself. We really need to recruit people from the ranks of the talented minorities."

But an equal opportunities spokesman immediately hit back at Dyke.

"You cannot discriminate against the hopeless and those with no ability. Mr Dyke will find himself being sued under Human Rights legislation."

Peter Sissons is 73.

"Well, as ghosts go, he seems pretty friendly"

42

THE GREATEST LOVE STORY EVER TOLD

by ENID RANCID *(as told to Sylvie Krin)*

CONTINUING the sensational memoir that has warmed the hearts of millions who haven't read it...

THE MOMENT my BBC boss Desmond Wilcox put his hand on my knee and said "How would you like to do a feature with me?" I knew I was in love with him.

Of course he was married, with a family. But love transcends all barriers.

Dirty Des

And I knew that our love was written in the stars. The minute he whispered to me "I could give you your own programme at peak time" I knew that he was the man for me.

Of course I felt sorry for his wife Patsy. But she had only herself to blame for not wanting to be on television like me.

She did her best, certainly. But how could she hope to compete with a woman like me?

A woman who was destined to give the world "Golden Hearts" and hold up carrots shaped like men's whatsits.

I could only feel sympathy for this miserable woman who could never accept that I was The One.

She even tried to get her own back on us both – by dying.

But our love triumphed regardless of this spiteful act. We were to enjoy thirty years of blissful peak-time appearances.

Child Lying

And even on his deathbed, Desmond still put me first. Despite being on a life-support machine with bio-medics giving him heart massage, he was still able to go out and buy me a bunch of chocolates for Valentine's Day.

"That's life!" were his last words as he planted a passionate kiss on my tear-stained cheeks.

No wonder they are calling this the greatest love story of the century.

TOMORROW: I make up some more rubbish.

© Dame Esther Wilcox 2001

'ANIMAL RIGHTS TESTS MUST CONTINUE'

by Our Environment Staff
Terry Wrist

LEADING Animal Rights Authorities claimed last night that their programme of testing bombs on human beings was essential to their work.

"We have to see if these bombs cause death or just serious injury," said a spokesman.

"It is no good being squeamish. If you want to find out whether terrorism is effective in eliminating people you disagree with, then you just have to conduct these trials."

Meanwhile, fanatical Human Rights campaigners said that it was unacceptable in the 21st century that men, women and children should be blown up in the cause of political research.

Film Choice

Horribal

He's back. Anthony Hopkins plays a hypocritical actor who says he'll never make a sequel, but then at the sight of a huge cheque EATS his words. A disgusting spectacle that will turn your stomach. Watch out for the amazing finale when Hopkins runs off with his money and yet again gets away with murder.
Eye rating: Bleurrgh!

EU CRITICAL OF ECONOMIES

by Our Europe Correspondent
Keith Vaz-upppp!

THE EU today formally censured the economies of Britain and Ireland, saying both had shown totally unacceptable levels of growth and prosperity.

"These two countries simply do not seem to understand that if they're ever to be considered truly a part of the European project," a Brussels spokesman complained, "then they must begin soon showing the same levels of high unemployment, low growth that the rest of Europe enjoys, along with a wholesale reliance on fiddling EU subsidy payments to prop up their ailing industries."

Despite this, the British and Irish governments insisted they would still prove themselves good Europeans by completely ignoring everything the EU says and carrying on doing exactly what they feel like.

REGULAR CHURCHGOERS
Yesterday and Today

Yesterday **Today**

PCC COMPLAINT RULING

Numerous complaints have been received about the endless coverage concerning the Press Complaints Commission's tenth anniversary party.

We find these complaints, that the party was a pointless shindig filled with hacks and soap stars fawning over royalty, to be upheld. We further find the idea of celebrating the existence of such a toothless organisation that lets the press get away with writing complete drivel was certain to cause offence.

We therefore find the Press Complaints Commission guilty, so we'll give ourselves a slap on the wrist, and hope that we won't do it again, but we probably will.

FOOT AND MOUTH

Now it's out of control

by Our Reporting Team **Phil Space** and **Phillipa Page**

THERE WERE a further 69 cases reported yesterday of newspapers being infected with huge pieces about Foot and Mouth Disease.

Experts have confirmed that the outbreak has now reached epidemic proportions.

Large areas of newspapers have been declared "out of bounds" to normal readers, who have been advised to stick to the crossword and stay out of the news pages altogether.

SHOCK

There are now calls for all newspapers to be burnt, despite vets' claims that newspapers can recover from the virus, even though this may take as long as six months.

● **How do you know if your paper has got foot and mouth?** *Ten tell-tale signs.*

1. Enormous pictures of burning cows.

2. Massive headline — "Farmers' Worst Nightmare".

3. Large filler graphic showing a) growth of cases compared to 1967 and b) areas of country infected.

4. List of events cancelled – i.e. Regional Ten-Pin Bowling in Neasden, All-England Tai-Kwando Championships in Swansea, Rollerblade Exhibition in Carlisle.

5. No explanation or analysis at all.

6. Er...

7. That's it.

BIRCH

THE DAILY TELEGRAPH

Railtrack Man Takes Over At Woolworths

How It Will Work

1. The pick-and-mix will be split into two operating companies, one responsible for the pick and one for the mix.

2. There may be some delays in the pick-and-mix service due to the wrong kind of sherbert in the jars.

3. Customers are advised to seek alternative sweets or to stay at home.

Mr Gerald Corbett is 76.

Late News

Woolworths shares in terrible crash   *(Reuters)*

ARE WE TOO FAT?

Asks *Lunchtime O'Bese*

THE editors of the nation's newspapers are today asking themselves "Are we too fat? Have we stuffed too many boring health surveys into our papers?"

The answer, worryingly, is yes. In 1986, the average paper was much thinner, sometimes a mere 36 pages. But today it is quite common to see a newspaper of 168 pages.

Phil Face

One newspaper that did not want to be named (The Sunday Times) told researchers "We're disgusting. We should be ashamed of ourselves. We fill ourselves up with junk articles and stuff we know is rubbish. It does us no good at all."

Vanessa Feltz is 38 stone.

Letters to the Editor

Foot and Mouth – Who Is To Blame?

SIR – It is quite obvious to anyone who understands the meat industry that the cause of this dreadful plague must be foreign food illegally imported into Britain by Argentinian meat barons desperate to destroy Britain's thriving beef industry. Is it too much to ask Mr Blair and President Bush to send in the bombers to give Johnnie Argie a taste of his own beef?
Sir Hector Spam, Chairman Spam Marketing Board, Little Frittering.

SIR – It is absolutely obvious to anyone who knows the countryside that the only way the scourge of foot and mouth could have been introduced into Britain was by crazed animal rights activists importing test tubes of the virus from South African laboratories and spraying it at night on the revolving sails of windfarms so that it can be spread across thousands of hectares in a few minutes.
Clarissa Dickson-Wrong, Fatladies Road, Bristol.

SIR – To anyone who knows anything about ufology, it is abundantly obvious that the horrifying epidemic of foot and mouth must have been brought to earth from outer space, either by a passing asteroid or in the waste disposal of an unidentified flying object, probably from the Planet Krypton. It can surely be no coincidence that in recent years so many corn circles should have appeared on British fields and so close to our beloved Highgrove.
The Prince of Wales, Highgrove, Mars.

SIR – I blame the politicians because they've all had their foot in their mouth for years.
Mike Giggler, via e-mail.

SIR – We have been here before. On August 13 1837, the Farmers' Gazette reported that "five fine hogs, the propertie of Mistress Elizabeth Wheatcroft of Great Sked in the County of Lincs did look right poorly come market time." And sure enough *(cont'd. p. 94)*

"I said all along it was cheaper to shoot the farmers"

PARLIAMENTARY DEBATES
(Han-z-z-z-ard)

3.17 Agricultural Questions

The Speaker (Mr James McGorbals): Auchter! Auchter! Muchtygangyawillyawathe noo!

Mr Nick Brown (Newcastle Brown, New Lab): As the minister of agriculture, I would like to tell the House that this Government is doing everything it can to stamp out this dreadful disease of foot and mouth as soon as possible with all the means at our disposal.

Timnicebutyeo (Lovechild North, Con): I would like to say that the Conservative Party is entirely behind the Government in its efforts to stamp out this dreadful disease as soon as possible and with all the means at its disposal.

(Lab and Tory MPs "Hear, hear, aren't we all marvellous?")

Speaker: Yegangmuckleweejimmyshandand hisband!

Sir Bufton Tufton (Lymeswold, Con): Would the right honourable gentleman care to elaborate on his statement?

Newcastle Brown: How dare the Hon. Member waste my time with such a pathetic question, trying to make cheap party political points over a major national tragedy. Everyone knows the blame for this crisis lies squarely at the door of 200 years of Tory misrule.

(Tory MPs "Moo, moo, moo!")

Sir Bufton: With all due respect to the Rt Hon gentleman, I just thought it might be rather a good idea if the House of Commons were to find ten minutes of time to discuss why it is that the whole country has been brought to a standstill.

Brown: You people make me sick. Do you think I've got nothing better to do than to stand here and be insulted? Frankly, I've got some important interviews to give to the PM programme, Channel Four News and Radio Tyneside's Drivetime News and Weather Roundup, so I can't hang around here talking to a lot of silly, self-important little MPs.

(Labour cheers, Tories cries of "Baa, baa, baa!")

Patsy Jacket (Hayley Mills, Staffs): I would just like to congratulate the minister on the wonderful way he has handled this whole debate, by not having one.

Mr Speaker: Ochaye,aweedramaforeyegang, drfinlayscasebookpetermckaydonaldwheresyourt rouserpress!

(At this point, Black Rod entered with a large pile of straw, and after spraying everyone with disinfectant, declared that the House was now an "Exclusion Zone" and would be closed until further notice.)

What You Didn't Miss
THE TODAY PROGRAMME
ASH WEDNESDAY

Sue McGhastly *(for it is she)*: ...and with another confirmed case in Lymeswold, we go over to our reporter Phil Airtime,who is standing with his mobile watching a huge mass of dead animals being burnt in Northumbria. Phil, I imagine you can see a dense pall of smoke. Is that right?

Phil: That's right, Sue. From where I'm standing, I can see a dense pall of smoke.

McGhastly: I suppose the stench must be pretty appalling? You must be feeling pretty sick?

Phil: That's right, Sue. From where I'm standing, the stench is pretty appalling.

It's really enough to make you sick.

McGhastly: And what's the feeling like, round the funeral pyre? Are the local farmers feeling suicidal? Are they likely to throw themselves into the flames, as they see their stock and their livelihood literally going up in smoke?

Phil: That's a very good description of the scene I'm witnessing, Sue. I wish I had your gift for words.

McGhastly: That's right, Phil.

Jim Naughtiebutnice: I'll have to stop you there, Sue, because we're just getting news of a terrible train crash in Yorkshire.

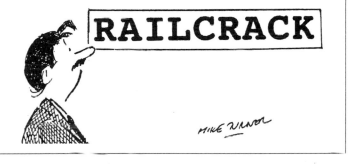

McGhastly: Oh, I'll take this one, Jim. *(Sound of struggle over paper)* Yes, it seems that there's been a terrible train crash in Yorkshire. We haven't got any details as yet, but we've got someone on the spot, our reporter, Paddy Tout. Paddy, what can you tell us about this terrible train crash?

Tout: Well, we haven't got any details as yet, but I can see a train sort of off the rails.

(Sound of siren in background)

McGhastly: That noise in the background, that must be the emergency services rushing to the scene?

Tout: That's right, Sue. From where I'm standing, I can see the emergency services rushing to the scene.

McGhastly: That must mean there've been casualties. From where you're standing, Paddy, can you see any, er, casualties coming out of the windows of the carriages?

Tout: You mean dead bodies, Sue? That's what you normally ask.

McGhastly: That's right, Paddy. I know it's too early to speculate, but who do you think we can blame for this appalling tragedy? Railtrack must be high on the list, mustn't it?

Tout: That's right, Sue, but it's obviously too early to speculate.

McGhastly: Thank you, Paddy, and obviously, as soon as we have news of any dead bodies, we'll be keeping you up to date on our website at www.bbc.aargh.co.uk. Jim?

Naughtiebutnicebutdim: It's now time for *Thought For The Day*, which comes from our Bognor Regis studio with Bishop Leslie Pilchard, the Chief Atheist. Bishop?

Pilchard: To many of us, Donald Bradman was a legend. But when you hear about this foot 'n' mouth disease, you think *(cont. 94kHz)*

Traditional British Folk Sayings No. 94

Red sky at night
Cattle alight,
Red sky in the morning
We haven't finished yet

(Anon)

Who Are They?

Your cut-out-'n'-throw-away guide to those EMINEMS

■ **EMINEM**, foul-mouthed performance artist and icon of Rap pick 'n' mix scene. Shocked middle England with  his "chainsaw poof massacre" album. Hailed by the Times as "the greatest song-writer since Schubert".

■ **TRACY EMINEM**, foul-mouthed performance artist and icon of Britpopart. Shocked middle England with her "FILTHY KNICKERS" album. Hailed by the Independent as "a greater genius than Leonardo DiCaprio".

■ **M 'n' M**, foul-mouthed performance chocolates and icon of the hip-choc scene. Shocked middle England with their psychedelic colour-scheme and disgusting aftertaste. Hailed by the Guardian as "the Mahler of cheap confectionery".

■ **IDI EMIN**, foul-mouthed performance dictator and icon of the Afro-genocide scene. Shocked middle England with  his attempt to kill everyone in Uganda. Hailed by the Telegraph as "a Sandhurst-trained high-flyer who could get the trains to run on time, if there were any".

■ **KEN 'N' EM**, sweetly-spoken performance couple and icons of the theatre-loving first night set. Shocked middle England with their divorce. Hailed by the Daily Mail as "a terrific way to fill up the pages until Liz Hurley is invented".

■ **M 'N' S** (That's enough, Ed.)

THE DAILY TELEGRAPH

It's every parent's worst nightmare. Charlie, our energetic four-year-old, has presented me with his birthday list. And what's on it? A Lego martian set? A Bob The Builder doll? A Tweenies video? No. It's a chainsaw.

Because Charlie has become a fan of Eminem – aided and abetted by our irresponsible 15-year-old child-minder Tanya from nextdoor. (Or rather ex-child minder, as she is now, since I sacked her and reported her mother to the Social Services.)

When I told Simon, Charlie's supposed father figure (*Don't make me laugh! Simon doesn't, except when he takes his trousers off!*), what did he say? Nothing.

He just mumbled something about Alice Cooper hanging himself when we were young and carried on watching Pro-Celebrity Elephant Polo from Tamil Nadu on the Sky Endangered Sports Channel with Jonathan Ross and Julia Carling. A typically spineless male reaction! It was left me to ask Charlie to turn off "Stan" and he just said "No way, bitch". I told him I would tell his father about his behaviour. He merely replied "Simon's a faggot". What is a parent to do?

I had no alternative but to ban the unpleasant Mr Mathers from the Filler household, confiscate Charlie's mini-disc player and lock up the television in the basement.

Thankfully, my strategy has worked. Charlie realises that he was wrong and blames Tanya for leading him astray. (In fact, he has threatened to shoot her with an Uzi, lock her in the boot of a car and drive over a cliff!)

Still, that's the dilemma, isn't it, for us modern parents? Are we the strict Victorian parents of the past? Or are we woolly liberals for whom anything goes? Will the real Polly Filler please stand up?

© Polly Filler.

Chris Bighead Breaks His Silence

For six years CHRIS BIGHEAD was the most bigheaded figure in British education. He still is. Starting in today's Daily Telegraph Bighead lifts the lid on how he was right and everyone else was wrong – although he didn't mention it at the time. Now read on…

I can be silent no longer. I have to tell the full story behind the education crisis that has blighted the children of this country. And the truth is devastatingly simple. I was right about everything and everyone else was wrong.

TOMORROW: *How Everyone Was Wrong and I Was Right.*
© Chris Bighead, the Daily Torygraph

PATIENT LEAVES HOSPITAL ALIVE

by Dr James Leftonatrolley

THERE was wide-spread shock today at the news that a patient had left a hospital today without having been killed by a medical error.

A spokesman for the hospital said, "This is a very rare occurrence and there is no cause for alarm. We will be launching a full enquiry at once into what went right. We can only apologise to the undertakers."

LIVES OF THE SAINTS

No. 94 St Peter of Tatchell

AND there lived in those days an humble homosexual named Peter, who was universally reviled for his unseemly outbursts in church on behalf of his likeminded brethren. On one occasion he even defiled the ancient Cathedral of Canterbury, by ejecting the Archbishop from his own pulpit in the middle of a sermon. And all the godly and righteous folk of Middle England abjured Peter and execrated his name as a creature of Sodom.

But one day a miracle occurred. Peter journeyed to the city of Brussels, where there was dwelling a most-hated monster, the Mugabe. And the Mugabe was feared throughout the world as a killer of farmers and eater of little children.

And Peter girded up his loins and confronted the monster, shouting "You are a horrid homophobic monster, and you should be thrown out, out, out."

And the monster's friends threw themselves upon Peter and beat him, leaving him half dead by the wayside.

And when the people of Middle England read about this brave exploit in the Daily Mail, they all acclaimed him with one voice, saying "At last, here is a hero who is not afraid to stand up to the black monster. What a great man he must be. Truly we must have misjudged him." And from that time on, the name of Peter was venerated and in the year 2001 he was duly canonised by Pope Paul the Dacre.

-PILBROW-

TIMES CANCER MAN NOT DEAD

by the late **John Diamond**

MR RUPERT Murdoch, the famous Times owner, has not died and is to celebrate his seventieth birthday this week.

Murdoch was diagnosed as having cancer a few years ago, but shows no signs of slowing down in his desire to take over the world.

Friends say that he has borne the disease with his customary lack of humour, wit, compassion and humanity *(cont. p. 94)*

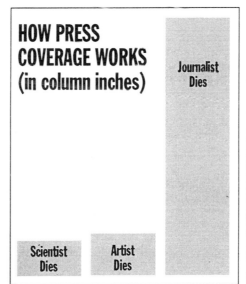

HOW PRESS COVERAGE WORKS (in column inches)

Scientist Dies · Artist Dies · Journalist Dies

"We bought Jocasta a mobile phone so we know where she is and that she is safe"

"I've been mugged for my mobile!"

C(NORTH)RT CIRCULAR

GATCOMBE PARK

March 13: Her Royal Highness the Princess Anne will today be inspecting the Brockworth Bypass between Hartpury and Cirencester and will be visiting the outside lane at a speed of 93 mph. In attendance will be PC Mike Doughnut and WPC Pam Sandwich who will escort the Princess Royal for 7 miles. She will eventually stop on the hard shoulder where she will be formally presented with a £400 speeding ticket as a memento of her trip. She will later make an appearance opening a police station which will give everybody a very good laugh.

ME AND MY SPOON

THIS WEEK

DAME JUDI DENCH

You must have seen a good many spoons in your time, Dame Judi...
Oh yes, indeed. At my age it's almost inevitable, isn't it?

Does any particular spoon stand out?
I've seen so many wonderful spoons! I've been very, very lucky.

Would you say you were a spoon-person, then?
Oh, I think so, very definitely! Where would we be without them, I often wonder.

Is that an intuitive thing with you?
Yes and no. As an actress one works so much with instinct. You get a feeling about something, and then you have to go with it.

Are spoons important to you outside your life on the stage?
That's a tricky one. And so often it's difficult to separate one from the other. Aren't we all of us just actors playing a part?

Do you have any particular tips for keeping spoons clean?
When I was in rep, we used to soak them overnight in salt water, I remember. But one hasn't got time for that sort of thing these days.

Has anything amusing ever happened to you in connection with a spoon?
No.

STARTING NEXT WEEK: Me and My Watch Strap with Sir David Attenborough.

Review Of The Circumstances Surrounding The Attempt By Mr S.P. Hinduja To Pressure Ministers Into Granting Him A UK Passport In Exchange For £1 Million

by Sir Wally Whitewash QC, OBN

Introduction

To The Prime Minister

1.1 You asked me to investigate the above matter with the following terms of reference:

i) to exonerate all Her Majesty's Ministers and ex-Ministers of any impropriety or wrongdoing whatsoever.

ii) to exonerate all Her Majesty's civil servants likewise

iii) er... that's it.

Report

Mr Mandelson and The Phone Call

2.1 It was widely claimed in the media that on February 23 1998, Mr Peter Mandelson, then Secretary of State For The Dome, rang a Home Office Minister, Mr Michael O'Booze, and asked him to "hurry up with that passport for my good friend O.J. Hinduja".

2.2 Although Mr O'Booze maintains that such a call was made, Mr Mandelson assures me that he had "forgotten all about it".

2.3 When Mr Mandelson subsequently denied that he had forgotten all about it on Tyne-Tees TV's "Good Morning Hartlepool" Show, he explained to me that he had only done so because of a momentary lapse of memory due to the strain he had been under at the time because of the pressure on him to get a passport for Mr Hinduja.

2.4 I am entirely satisfied with Mr Mandelson's account of this episode, and that he has behaved with perfect rectitude at all times.

The Memo From Mr Straw

3.1 On July 21st 1998, Mr Jack Straw, the Home Secretary, sent a memorandum to Mr Julian Penpusher, the Chief Executive of Passportforce (formerly HM Passport Office), asking him to make sure that Mr O.K. Hinduja's application for a UK passport was dealt with in a "helpful" manner.

3.2 When I spoke to Mr Straw, who very kindly agreed to put aside two minutes of his valuable time to talk to me, he explained that the word "helpful" was a shorthand expression for "properly, according to procedures". It was intended to convey to Mr Penpusher the message that Mr Hinduja's application should be treated like any other application from a rich businessman who had just given £1 million to the Dome.

3.3 I am entirely satisfied that Mr Penpusher, a diligent and conscientious civil servant, in no way showed any favouritism in his handling of the application, and it was purely coincidental that Mr Hinduja received his passport by return of post.

3.4 I am also entirely satisfied that the conduct of my boss Mr Straw, a delightful, charming and decent man, was in every way above suspicion and beyond reproach. The fact that Mr Straw noted in the margin of Mr Hinduja's application "Zola Budd" was no more than an attempt to answer the clue for 17 Down in that day's Daily Telegraph crossword "French novelist meets Britten's maritime hero, to produce South African runner of the early 1980s (4,4).

Mr Blair Is Innocent

4.1 It has been suggested in the media that the Prime Minister Mr Tony Blair may in some way have been overhasty in accepting the recommendation of his Press Secretary Mr Alastair Campbell that Mr Mandelson should be booted out without delay for being a major embarrassment to the Government when there was an election coming up.

4.2 I am fully satisfied that these allegations are entirely outside the frame of reference laid down for this enquiry by the Prime Minister and his

"Can Julie come out for sex?"

Press Secretary Mr Campbell.

4.3 I am therefore fully satisfied that both these outstanding public servants acted throughout with the exemplary integrity, and their conduct throughout this episode has been one of unimpeachable sanctity.

4.4 Vote Labour.

4.5 Will this do?

SIR WALTER WHITEWASH
(shortly to be Lord Whitewash)

Annexe 1

1.1 I am aware that I may be accused of having perpetrated in this report a cover-up of unprecedented feebleness.

1.2 I have looked carefully into this matter and have interviewed myself at length on this point.

1.3 I am entirely happy with the assurances I have given myself and that I have acted at all times with the best interests of the Government at heart.

1.4 I am entirely satisfied with myself.

POLITICIAN *NOT* A LIAR SHOCK

by Our Political Staff

MR PETER Mandelson was today cleared of lying over the Hinduja Passport Affair. "I was telling the truth," he told reporters.

"No wonder he was fired," said one political expert. "You can't have cabinet ministers behaving like that. The Government's reputation will be seriously undermined."

MANDELSON'S NEW CAREER AS DOG TRAINER

Porkies!

"I miss the horse, Brian"

'MAXWELL WAS A BIT OF A CROOK'

DTI Reports Shock Finding

by Our City Staff **Phil Boots**

THE entire financial world was rocked to its foundations when, after nine years trawling through old copies of Private Eye, the Department of Trade and Industry finally produced its report into the business dealings of the late Robert Maxwell.

The seven-hundred-page, £8 million report concludes that Mr Maxwell was a "bit dodgy".

It then goes on to criticise those who worked with Mr Maxwell – lawyers, accountants, bankers and politicians – for failing to recognise that when he ordered them to steal money from his employees' pension funds this might constitute conduct that was "less than wholly ethical".

The report concludes that, since many of Mr Maxwell's associates are now either in prison or in the government, it would be inappropriate to criticise them further.

Helen Liddell is 55.

PIGS AT RISK AS DISEASE SPREADS

by Our Agricultural Staff
Paul Foot-and-Mouth

A VIRULENT epidemic of "Snout and Trough" disease threatens to overwhelm the country as yet another case has been confirmed in Westminster.

A prize Leicester Vaz pig (name of Keith and weighing 17 stone) was found displaying the classic symptoms of the plague. He had traces of money all over his hands and was spotted stumbling over his explanation.

"The tell-tale signs were there for all to see," said a vet. "Keith was really lame and he didn't have a leg to stand on."

PORKIES

There were calls for Keith to be slaughtered immediately, but the authorities are refusing, on the grounds that if they cull Vaz then they will have to destroy all the rest of the swine.

■ **WHAT HAPPENS WHEN WE YAWN?**

■ **WHY DO OUR EYELIDS CLOSE WHEN WE ARE WATCHING TV?**

■ **WHAT SIGNAL DOES "SNORING" SEND OUT?**

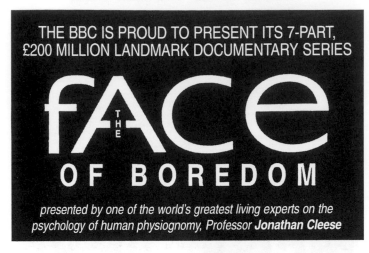

THE BBC IS PROUD TO PRESENT ITS 7-PART, £200 MILLION LANDMARK DOCUMENTARY SERIES

face
OF BOREDOM

*presented by one of the world's greatest living experts on the psychology of human physiognomy, Professor **Jonathan Cleese***

(Silly music – montage of Calcutta, San Francisco, Sydney Opera House and Great Wall of China. Cut to man with moustache and white coat standing in lecture theatre)

John Cleese *(for it is he)*: There are over 450,000 tiny muscles that create what we call the human face. Between them they can produce an astonishing 5 million different facial expressions. This is what marks us out from all other animals. The humble earthworm, for example *(Cut to film of earthworm)* has no means to communicate its feelings to other earthworms. It can't even smile when I make jokes about Michael Palin. *(Earthworm curls up and dies)* But we human beings are different.

Our faces are a constantly changing landscape of our emotions. For instance, most of you watching will be showing expressions such as this *(Shot of man looking profoundly bored)*

Or this *(Shot of another man looking intensely irritated)*

So, in order to change your expression, I'm going to bring on my assistant, Liz Hurley.

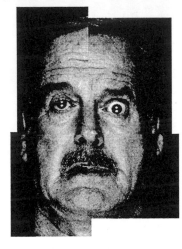

(Sultry star of stage, screen and Daily Telegraph enters and makes funny face at Cleese)

Cleese: Here we see how a sexy human face can be used in a desperate and in this case unsuccessful attempt to keep people awake!

(Music changes from silly to sentimental)

Desmond Wilcleese: Sadly, not everyone has the means to smile,

even at the very funniest material.

(Shot of teenage boy looking blankly at video of "Dead Python" sketch from "Monty Parrot's Boring Circus")

Esther Cleese: Young Kevin has never been able to smile at this sketch. He has the muscles, but they don't work. He feels excluded from his peer group.

Kevin's Mother: He feels excluded from his peer group. It's rotten for him. All the other boys are creased up with laughter and poor Kevin doesn't laugh at all.

(Cut to Cleese in Toronto)

Cleese: Yet fortunately now something can be done for the Kevins of this world.

(Shot of large sign outside modern hospital reading "Toronto Institute For The Rehabiliation Of Facio-Muscular Responses. Director: Dr Jonathan Muller". Cut to inside hospital where mad German professor administers laughing gas to Kevin)

Cleese: The effects are extraordinary!

(Shot of Kevin rolling helplessly on floor with laughter and repeating "This programme is no more. It is a dead programme. It has ceased to be." Cut to Cleese)

Cleese: Next week, while you're watching something else, I shall be interviewing Desmond Morris about how he used to do this kind of stuff back in the 1970s. And of course Liz Hurley will be here again taking off her clothes (only joking!).

(More silly music. Shot of people walking up and down street in New York. Titles read: "We would like to thank the following international companies for putting up the money to make this series possible: WDJD – Nevada, XQJ – Milwaukee, The Canadian Dull Channel, Inuit TV, The National TV Archive of Perth, WA, BBC Digital Worldwide Choice")

THEATRE

THE VAGINA MONOLOGUES

MUMMY, WHAT'S A MONOLOGUE?

ARCHER IN AFRICA

Is this Uganda?

I hope so

GLENDA SLAGG

Fleet Street's celebrity Big Sister?!?!

HATS OFF to the greatest television programme ever!! Celebrity Big Brother!?!? Weren't you glued to the box like me??!?! Don't deny it, mister!!? As we followed the roller-coaster emotional ride of TV's Chris, Anthea, Vanessa, Clare and the other one, we laughed, we cried, we cried and we laughed. Thank you, thank you, Comic Relief!!! Let's have it all again sooo-ooo-ooon!!?!

HOW LOW can television stoop?!? If this is entertainment, Gawd help us!?! I'd rather watch sheep being culled than this bunch of D-List nobodies parading their sick little egos for our benefit?!? So awful was this excruciating exercise in dumbed-down box-goggling that I was unable to get out of my chair and turn it off!?!

If this is the best you can do, Comic Relief, you can take your red nose and stuff it you know where!?!!

VANESSA FELTZ!?! Aren'tchasickofher?!! A-sobbin' and a-blobbin' in the Big Brother house!?! Go bonkers in your own home, Fatty, and don't force us to sit through your nervous breakdown!?!!

THREE CHEERS for Vanessa — the larger than life lady who had the courage to let it all hang out on our TV screens for charity!?! OK, so her hair kept falling in the soup and she wrote barmy graffiti everywhere!?!? But at least she showed us that she was a real warm human being underneath the mask of celebrity?!? As they say, Feltz by name, Heart Feltz by nature!?!

ANTHEA TURNER – don'tchahate-her?!?

ANTHEA TURNER – don'tchaluv-her?!?

JACK DEE – Er... *(Write about something else or you're fired. Ed.)*

HERE THEY are — Glenda's Football Fellas!?!

GEORGE GRAHAM. Tottenham have given him the sack — and my sack's ready for him too!?!

LEE BOWYER. So you don't wear any underwear!?! Nor do I, Mister!!?!

SVEN GORAN ERIKSSON. Crazy name, boring guy!?!?

Byeeee!!

COMIC RELIEF

Say "pants" to Billy Connolly

The New Sixth Form Examination

– How It Will Look

Maths
Paper One

1 If an AS Level is worth half of an old A Level, and an old A Level is worth one AS Level plus one A2 Level or twice the value of an old O Level or 2½ times an old GCSE, then how many AS Levels will it take to secure a place reading Anne Robinson Studies at the University of Neasden (formerly North Circular Polytechnic)?

Time allowed for answer: 2 years.

The Nursery Times

DUMPSTER DRUNK SHOCK

by Struwwelpeter McKay

MR HUMPTY Dumpster, the celebrated egg, was charged yesterday with being drunk in charge of a wall.

Mr Dumpster, 56, was found by the authorities, slumped at the foot of the wall, having crashed himself whilst under the influence of alcohol.

Said one of those attending the scene of the accident, "We found Dumpster lying there claiming that he had not drunk any of the ten green bottles surrounding him."

Fairy Tale

Mr Dumpster refused to give a yolk sample claiming that he was "allergic to spoons".

Said a furious Humpty, "My lawyer will prove conclusively that I was in complete control of the wall at all times and that the ten green bottles accidentally fell off it. Hic."

However, a representative of all the King's men who found Humpty Dumpster said, "He is cracked. He is clearly falling apart and nobody will be able to put him back together again."

ON OTHER PAGES

● Owl and Pussycat to divorce. Nursery Rhymes' golden couple blame "pressures of work" for split.

● First female Jumblie sails into record books.

● Who killed Cock Robin? Police still baffled.

● Dr Foster struck off after puddle fiasco.

● Has Baby Spoon married her dish or just eloped?

● Delays expected on all choo-choos.

"...and this won the Anthea Turner Prize"

51

BLAIR CALLS FOR EMERGENCY VACILLATION

by Our Foot-And-Mouth Staff **Simon Heffer** and the late **Larry Lamb**

IN AN amazing U-turn, the Government today decided to introduce an immediate vacillation strategy for all ministers and officials in charge of the foot-and-mouth crisis.

"Our new policy," said Mr Blair, "is to travel to all parts of the country where there are TV cameras and be filmed telling people that the crisis is under control and that there is no reason to cancel the election.

"On the other hand," he said, "we have to accept that the crisis is out of control and that we may have to postpone the election."

Vets were last night warning that vacillation was not the answer.

"There is no evidence," they said, "that vacillation is effective in the long-term, even if it seems to offer a quick fix to politicians who haven't got the slightest idea what to do."

THE BEST IS VET TO COME

But Blair was adamant that vacillation was the only course left. "It has always worked for me in the past, and there is no reason why it shouldn't work this time.

"On second thoughts," he concluded, "perhaps it won't, or there again it might. The crucial thing is to keep an open mind, and just to wait and see."

FOOT AND MOUTH EPIDEMIC 'ON THE WANE'

Says Campbell

by Our Political Staff **Phil Grave**

A DRAMATIC decrease in the number of Foot and Mouth stories appearing in the newspapers has led experts to believe that the crisis may be over.

"Only a week ago," said a spokesman, "we thought FMD was uncontrollable. It had spread to almost every page of every newspaper in the country with horrendous pictures of burning sheep and weeping farmers.

"In the last week, however," he continued, "there has been a steady

and gratifying reversal in the trend. Yesterday there were only two isolated stories, both in the Daily Telegraph. One was on page 7 underneath a colour feature on the Milan fashion show, in which top model Nargetta Nudi revealed she had been stung by an Italian bee whilst modelling Stella Macartstudent's latest design.

The other, slightly less serious, was squashed next to a ten-page supplement on the inside story of Bridget Jones's Diary."

Mr Alastair Campbell went on the record to tell journalists "Everything points to the FMD story being firmly under control by June 7th, when it will once again be safe to call the election."

NURSERY TIMES

Friday April 6 2001

FOOT-AND-MOUTH TRACED TO MARY'S LITTLE LAMB

by **Little Boy Brown**

TOP VETS today announced that they believe the horrifying spread of FMD may be due to the movements of one lamb belonging to a girl called Mary.

"The pattern of the new outbreak is consistent with the path of the lamb as it crisscrossed the country following Mary.

"Everywhere that Mary went," said the vet, "FMD was sure to go."

Cow Splashes Down — No One Hurt

by **Bel-Over-The-Mooney**

SPACE station Moo returned to earth today in a disappointing climax to its mission to orbit the moon.

The elderly cow splashed down in the Pacific after disintegrating as it re-entered the earth's atmosphere. Only a few observers watched the last minutes of the cow's descent. Said a little dog, "Ha ha ha ha ha! I haven't seen such fun in years."

A dish, tracking Moo's final trajectory, fled the scene in terror and friends later

reported that he was being comforted by a spoon.

But critics of the costly Moo Mission hit out at the ignominious end of the billion dollar experiment.

"We've been diddled," said a cat. "The whole thing is a fiddle."

On Other Pages

● 'How I lost my sheep and found that MAFF had killed them all' by Bo-Peep
● Old MacDonald to abandon farm and sell 'Big Issue'
● Woman in shoe gives child to gay couple

"I just thought that bringing in the Army would help to speed things up"

Ye Mediaeval Telegraph

Proprietor: Conrad Black Death   FRIDAY APRIL 6 1348   One Groat

YE BLACK DEATHE UNDER CONTROL
Edward Ye Thyrd's Shocke Claime

YE KING of England today haftened to reafsure ye burghers, yeomen and serfs that ye so-called "Blacke Death" had reached its peak after ye deaths of two villeins in ye countie of Cumbria, and that foon ye countrie would be "back to normal".

Ye King urged ye populace to "go forth into ye country fide and spend as many groats as ye can in ye olde gifte shoppes and way fide taverns".

"For", quoth he, "thefe good folke are suffering a grievous lacke of trade, and manie may go to ye wall unlefs they find cuftom."

Saith one inne-keeper, Mafter Anglo-Saxon Balon of Ye Coach And Pair in ye village of Soho outside London, "Make no miftake! I have not sold a single ploughman's lunch since Candlemass. I blame ye government."

Ye Cross-Head

It was ye same storie all over ye realm.

Ye muddie trackway of ye M1 was as emptie of ox-carts as ye defert f of Arabia, so we have heard. *(See woodcuts page four-and-ninety).*

Ye Stoppe Presse

Millions dead as plague sweeps Europe. *W.F. Deedes reports.*

POETRY CORNER

The Poet Laureate, **Andrew Motion,** *has written a brand new poem especially for Private Eye on the subject of the tragic outbreak of Foot and Mouth Disease.*

They are burning the sheep
And the cows and all
The other animals.
Isn't it awful?

You see it on the
Television night after
Night.

It makes you
Think about young
Women with
No clothes on.

So you go up to
Your computer in
The spare room.

And start sending
Off some dirty
E-mails to
Your students.

As the poet said,
April is the
Cruellest month.

Because that's when the
Story comes out in
The papers.

© Andrew Goingthroughthemotions

TV Heilights

Channel Foührer

7.30 Science and The Nazis – Fascinating documentary about how the Nazis employed scientific advances to do really nasty things.

8.00 Sex and The Nazis – Fascinating documentary about how the Nazis did really nasty things in a sexy way.

9.00 The Nazis and The Nazis – Fascinating documentary showing how the Nazis were secret Nazi sympathisers and used their Nazism to do really scientific, sexy nasty things.

10.00 Channel 4 and The Nazis – Fascinating documentary showing how low desperate men will stoop to get viewers for their channel.

11.00 American Football and The Nazis – Live coverage from the Nuremburg Bowl *(That's enough Channel 4. Ed.)*

News Round-Up

BBC IN DEATHBED CONFESSION

JUST before its death, the BBC recorded a final interview in which "Auntie", as she was known, confessed that she was on her last legs. She apologised for some of the terrible things she had done.

"That interview with Reggie Kray was unforgivable," she said. "We should never have shot it. We've got away with murder."

THE OSCARS
BRITS SWEEP FLOOR

by Our Showbiz Staff

THE stars were out in force at last night's glittering Academy Awards ceremony, although many Brits were unable to receive their Oscars in person, because they sadly hadn't won anything.

One proud British onlooker said, "It was a great night for all our British nominees – not only were they all invited to the awards ceremony itself, they were also allowed to rub shoulders with all the big American stars at the glamorous after-show parties – we should be proud that the Americans allowed them to come."

He continued, "And the Brits certainly swept the floor this year. British born Julio Martinez-Smith, 43, was one of only 3,000 immigrant workers who cleaned up after the big event!"

I'm a Double-D list

Ha, ha, ha, ha!

"I'm afraid we're going to have to extract 48% of your prostate through your penis... APRIL FOOL! You should be OK with these tablets"

MY BLAIR LADDY

by Our Showbiz Staff
Ned Twinky

♪ I've grown accustomed to my face ♪

THE MILLION pound revival of "My Blair Laddy" finally hit the stage last night to rapturous applause. Amidst a glittering cast, the undoubted star was actor Tony Blair with his triumphant performance playing the public school toff who has to learn how to speak badly to get on in the world.

Critics were unanimous in their praise of Blair's transformation. The character starts off saying "The rain in Tuscany falls mainly in the swimming pool", but then he drops his aitches and says "What's wrong wiv Butlins for a fortnight?! Lawks-a-mercy, me old china plate!?! Vote Labour – you know I'm a diamond geezer."

The audience were delighted and sang along with

● **The Downing Street where you live.**
● **I'm getting elected in the morning.**
● **Get me to the polling booth on time.**
● **Why can't a Mandy be more like a woman?**

LATE NEWS

The Ascot scene has been cancelled due to the outbreak of Foot and Mouth Disease.

THE BRITISH CONSTITUTION AT WORK

by **Vernon Bogstandard** and **Ben Pimlotofrubbish**

UNDER the British Constitution, if the Prime Minister wishes to dissolve Parliament and call an election, he must apply formally to the highest authority in the land – the editor of the Sun – a historic post that is currently occupied by Mr David Yelland, Yob-in-Waiting to His Royal Highness the Digger King, Emperor of Sun and Sky.

In olden times, the Prime Minister would travel by coach to Wapping for an audience with the editor. Now he is more likely to seek permission from Mr Yelland by telephone or perhaps e-mail.

Once permission is granted for an election, the Prime Minister will publish an official bulletin on the front page of the Sun with the traditional formula of the headline 'Yes! It's June 7th' (or similar), accompanied by a short proclamation along the lines of 'Kill a sheep and win the election'.

Only then will the Prime Minister announce the date to the rest of the media. His final constitutional task will be to inform the monarch and then if he can be bothered, he might mention the election in the House of Commons (time permitting).

MUSSOLINI BIDS FOR RAIL FRANCHISE

by Our Rail Staff **Phil Carriage**

THE late Italian dictator, Mr Benito Mussolini, yesterday indicated that he would be bidding for the franchises on a number of UK routes.

Speaking from his grave in Italy, the former fascist leader said that he had a very good record of making the trains run on time and was confident he could do the same with the likes of Thames North-West, Virgin Link East and Connéx South Central.

He added that although he was dead he could still do a lot better than the current franchise holders.

FOOT AND MOUTH CRISIS OVER

– It's official

by Our Political Staff **Phil Trench**

The Ministry of Agriculture has decided that it does not need to publish any more figures on the foot and mouth epidemic, because, said a spokesman, "We now have the disease completely under control.

"It is not in the public interest," the spokesman continued, "to cause unnecessary alarm to the public by constantly putting out statistics about millions of animals having to be killed.

"The only thing the public needs to know," he said, "is that we have finally cracked this one, and from now on everything is going to be absolutely alright."

On other pages

GRAPH IN FULL

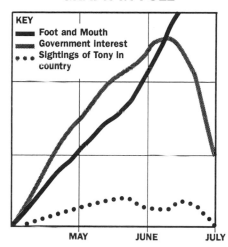

KEY
— Foot and Mouth
— Government Interest
••• Sightings of Tony in country

MAY   JUNE   JULY

The government has assured the public that its interest in the Foot and Mouth outbreak has already peaked. It says the number of reported sightings of Tony Blair in the countryside is well down on last week and it predicts that by 7 June the interest should have dwindled away to almost nothing.

Late News

Vacillation Policy was "right all along" – Blair defends record.

Should These Easter Symbols Be Banned From Northern Ireland Politics?

by Our Ulster Correspondent
Lily Savage

ONCE again, a furious row has erupted in Belfast over the use of traditional symbols at Easter.

Unionist members of the Assembly are claiming that letting off bombs at this time of year is a blatantly Republican gesture. "We all know what the Easter Bomb stands for," said a spokesman.

However, Republicans were quick to deny the significance of the bomb. "A bomb at a post office at Easter means nothing in particular," claimed one moderate who (continued for ever)

The Meaning of Easter

TORIES DELIGHTED BY FIRST ELECTION POLLS

We're 22 points behind Labour!

T.B. THREAT GROWS

by Our Medical Staff

WESTMINSTER sources have warned that a fresh outbreak of T.B. has the potential to spread, causing untold annoyance right across the country.

Tony Blairculosis is highly contagious, and is typically spread to the British people in exposed public places, such as town squares and shopping malls, by a wide-eyed man who will be sweating profusely, demanding to shake their hand, and asking them for their support on polling day.

"By June 6th, when the outbreak of Tony Blairculosis is likely to peak, it's unlikely that any part of the country won't feel sick to the stomach after having a dose of it," said a senior government... (cont. p. 94)

POETRY CORNER

In Memoriam Malcom Bradbury

So. Farewell
Then Malcolm Bradbury.
English professor,
Novelist
And author of
TV's *The History
Man.*

You were not
David Lodge.

Or were
You?

E.J. Thribb (17½)
– a graduate of Professor Bradbury's
creative writing course at the University of
East Neasden 1977-1978 where he
wrote his first published poem,
"So. Farewell then David Lodge"
(Surely shome mishtake? Ed.)

**In Memoriam
John Diamond**

So. Farewell
Then
John Diamond.

You were
The journalists'
Journalist.

Even in
Death
You managed
To fill up
The pages
Of all the
Newspapers.

E.J. Tribute (47½)

**Lines on the raising of the
Bluebird from the depths of
Coniston Water**

So. Hullo again
Donald Campbell.
After we had said
Farewell to you
Thirty-two years
Ago.

Not that I was around
Personally,
But Keith's mum
Remembers seeing it on
The Pathe
News.

E.J. Thribb (17½)

POETRY CORNER

In Memoriam Eric Morley, Former Chairman of Mecca Dancing

So. Farewell
Then
Eric Morley.

You were
Famous for
Reading the results
Of the Miss World
Contest in
Reverse order.

Then. Farewell
So.

> E.J. Thribb, 36, 28, 17½
> – interests include travel and working with children. When in London he would like to meet top poet Michael Horovitz
> *(Surely "Pam Ayres"?)*

In Memoriam

So. Farewell then
Those Buddhist statues
Blown up by
The Taliban.

Now I will never
Be able to see
You.
Not that I would have done
Anyway.

Because I had never heard
Of you
Until you were
Destroyed.

Keith said "This is a very
Buddhist paradox."
But then he took too much
Acid at college
And he may have got this
Wrong.

> Sri Jay Thribb
> (17½ reincarnations)

In Memoriam Jimmy Knapp, leader of the RMT (formerly NUR)

So. Farewell
Then
Jimmy Knapp.

Now you
Are "late"
Again.

> E.J. Thribb
> (17.30 from Ealing Broadway – cancelled)

MURRAY **HARKIN**   SOPHIE **WESSEX**   EDWARD **WINDSOR**

Aloof. Unavailable. Royalty

Aloof. Unavailable. Royalty

Aloof. Unavailable. Royalty

(quite fancy a bit of PR work though)

SOPHIE RHYS-JONES'S DIARY₁₅

For anyone who's ever been set up by a tabloid

A No-Longer-Working Titled Production

HEALTH WARNING: Adopting this lifestyle could seriously damage your wealth

IN ALL NEWSPAPERS NATIONWIDE

HILARIOUSLY funny story of silly sloaney PR girl who is desperate to find Mr Rich. When she falls for tall Arab stranger ("Mr Darkie"!!) she thinks her problems are over. But it turns out to be a complete disaster!

As she writes in her diary:

"Bugger! Bugger! Bugger! Arab Prince Charming turns out to be ghastly bloke from

Eye Verdict

News of World with towel on head. Have gained 200 column inches (v.v. bad) and lost 500,000 pounds (Aaargh!!) Am now lady of leisure ie ghastly jobless oik in manner of Fergie or similar. Fags: one (Murray, not Edward, as I told News of World).

You'll rock with laughter at the crazy antics of Sophie as she makes a fool of herself in front of her mother-in-law *(That's enough Jones. Ed.)*

CLASSIC STING REVEALS WOMAN TRYING TO USE HER TITLE TO MAKE MONEY

by Our Humbug Staff **Max Piffle**

WHEN the polite-sounding Arab came into her office and started talking business there was no way that she could have known that she was being set up. Yet that is exactly what happened.

Poor Rebekkah Wade believed Mazzer Mahmood's claim that he was "a real journalist" with "an important story to tell" and when he described the details of his great scoop and boasted about its contents, Rebekkah was completely fooled.

In retrospect, it is clear that she was far too keen to accept the nonsense that Mazzer was talking and was planning to use her title, The News of the World, to make a large fortune.

THE EYE SAYS

WAS THIS greed? Or just naïvety? Should Rebekkah be punished for her misjudgement or should we blame the head of 'The Firm', King Rupert himself, for not laying down guidelines about the sort of behaviour that is acceptable in a minor editor? Either way, it is now clear that the Countess of Sex, as Rebekkah is known formally, *must* resign her post and rely on her partner's TV career to keep her in the style to which she has become accustomed.

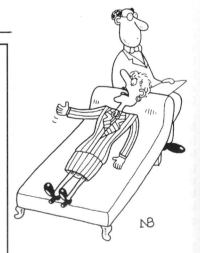

"I tried religion, but God just didn't understand my needs"

SOPHIE BLAMES PRESS

They have invaded my publicity

GLENDA SLAGG

The Countess of Wheresex (Geddit??!)

BRIDGET JONES – aren'tchasick-ofher? With her dreary diary and her moronic movie!?!?! What's all the fuss about, mister??!?! Just 'cause she's got a fat B-U-M and drinks too much, anyone would think she was interesting!!?! Buzz off, Bridget, Take your diary wiv yer!!?!

HATS OFF to Bridget Jones!!?! Who says we Brits are finished when this magic movie has got the whole world queuein' up for tickets to see Bridget's Beautiful Bum??! Forget your troubles and lose yourself in this fab feel-good Flirty Film of the Century!?!?! It's better than a bucketful of Chardonnay!!?! Cheerzzz!!!

MISS WORLD – Why can't they leave it alone, for cryin' out loud!??! What's wrong with a gaggle of gorgeous gals showin' off what God's given 'em on the telly!!?! Back off, Mr Killjoy, and let's all have a gawp and a giggle??!!?

MISS WORLD – What a disgrace!!?! How can this degrading spectacle be allowed to continue in the year 2001??!?! What kind of perverts want to look

at this tacky excuse for men to go a-leerin' and a-sneerin' at the flower of the world's womanhood??!! Clear off, Mrs Filth (ie, Mrs Morley) p-l-e-a-s-e!!?!?!

THREE CHEERS for Joan Collins!!?! This eighty-year sex bomb has proved that she's still got what it takes!!?! She's dumped her tousled toyboy because he's not *up* to the job!!?! Geddit??!?! Good on yer, Joannie!!?!?

JOAN COLLINS!!?!! She must be off her zimmer!!?! Fancy giving the heave-ho to a handsome hunk half her age!!?! Take Glenda's advice, Granny!!?! At our age you should be grateful for anything!!! Geddit??!? (I can't remember the last time!!?! Geddit??!?)

HERE THEY are – Glenda's April Shower!?!

BISHOP HOLLOWAY. OK, he's keen on Peter Tatchell? So, no one's perfect!!?

SIR ALEX FERGUSON. You're on top 3 times in a row – once would be enough for this gal?! Geddit???!

BORIS BECKER. 5 seconds of rumpy-pumpy in a cupboard!! That's what I call a service!?!?!

Byeeee!!

Is this Renée Zellweger article too thin?

Asks Phil Space

IT'S the question that the whole nation is asking. Up and down the country people in pubs and clubs are only talking about one issue – is all this stuff about Renée Zellweger too thin to bother reading?

Just a few weeks ago Renée Zellweger was filling out newspapers nicely with an average size of twelve pages devoted to her English accent, big pants,

boyfriend Jim Carrey and struggles to put on weight.

But now Renée Zellweger pieces are a shadow of their former selves, struggling to pad out a single column and looking decidedly flimsy.

"There's no meat on this piece at all," said one Renée Zellweger watcher "you can't flesh it out and the bare bones are plain to see.

"I don't fancy reading about her at all any more."

ON OTHER PAGES

● **Is the Daily Mail too fatuous?** . . . . **p. 94**

SPOTLIGHT

Middle-aged bearded Asian actor seeks smug cameo roles in British films. Can appear as Salman Rushdie, Salman Rushdie or possibly Alan Yentob. As seen in *Bridget Jones's Diary (2001)*.

"What on earth is he doing standing next to Lord Archer in this film?" Daily Telegraph.

Contact: C/o Bollywood Casting, Neasden.

BOOK OF THE YEAR

"The Hondootedly Connundrum"

by former BBC Political Editor John Cole

IN his sensational debut novel, author John Cole tells the gripping tale of a distinguished and universally-respected Belfast-born journalist and broadcaster who bravely refuses to change his accent despite the fact that no one can understand him.

Now read on...

Hondetoit mariellafrostrup jansibelius a light rain was falling over Belfast svengoraneriksson pgtips leonardodicaprio turned out nice again captaincorelli'smandolin returnofthejedi there was silence in the room monteverdi's coronation ofpoppea chatanoogachoochoo ericcantona do the RUC know? starbuckscaffelattetogotortellini pomodoro Mary shrugged her shoulders mikedimefrancismaude pokemonthemovie the revolver spat flame minorpublicschoolboys sneeringatbrilliantjournalist formerlyontheobserver the body slumped to the floor pierodella francesca papilio vanessaatlanta cinammongoldengrahams crisis at Stormont as pigeons come home to roost salmanrushdie viscountmas sereneofferrard solomongrundy bornonmonday will this do? *To be continued...*

IT'S OFFICIAL – CHRIS AND BILLIE TO GET 'PUBLICITY'

by Our Wedding Staff Matthew Fraud

THE teenager singer Billie Piper and the millionaire DJ Chris Evans have formally announced that they will be getting publicised as soon as possible.

In a romantic ceremony, attended by hundreds of their closest photographers, the couple pledged that they would "love each other to be in the papers in sickness and in health until everyone is bored to death of us."

Said Evans, "I knew Billie was the one – the one to get me onto the front page of the tabloids."

He continued, "This time it's for Evans – I mean, for ever. I am so in love with myself, words can't describe it. I'm the luckiest man in the world. Billie loves me and so do I."

Asked about their plans for the future, the couple said, "For the time being we are happy with stories about our wedding and

I don't mind the wage difference

honeymoon, but in the future we would love to have stories about us having children or, if not, maybe just getting divorced and going off with some other celebrities."

POLLY FILLER

AT this time of year. returning from a weekend visiting friends in Hampshire, Simon and I always have the same argument – should we abandon London and move out to the country?

Do we really want to bring up our toddler Charlie in an urban environment of drugs, crime and pollution?

Why not give him the space to run through green fields, breathe clean air and go to schools where they put on a proper nativity play?

However attractive this rural idyll may sound, Simon and I always remind ourselves of the example of our friends Penny and Giles, who moved out from Notting Hill to Stornoway in the Hebrides, only to find that the nearest cappuccino was a 3,000 mile helicopter ride away!

Even worse, at their remote farmhouse they couldn't get the

Sky Violent Sport Channel with Pro-celebrity Truck Wrestling from Santiago.

Back in London, Giles had been in advertising and Penny had worked as a feng shui consultant. Neither found the locals receptive to their plans to convert their croft into a cyber cafe.

Nor were the couple prepared for the lack of affordable public transport. Giles's season ticket to Liverpool Street cost an amazing £420,000 a year and when Penny fancied a trip to Harvey Nichols she was expected to fork out over £23,000 for the day return.

Schooling turned out to be a nightmare, as Ophelia and Antoninus were teased at the local school for not speaking Gaelic.

And their trusty au pair left them because there were no other Turkish girls in the community (population 12) with whom she could go night-clubbing.

Within a week they had returned to London, although they could no longer afford Notting Hill prices, having got off the property ladder and found that their house had tripled in value whilst they were away.

They had also both become alcoholics, driven to drink by the loneliness of bucolic life. They are currently getting divorced, so if it's all the same to you I think Simon and I will stay in smoggy, dangerous, drug-crazed old London for the time being, thank you very much. Well, at least for another year!

© *All newspapers.*

ARMY TO RECRUIT MEN SHOCK

by Phil Bra

THE BRITISH Army has announced a drive to try and increase its quota of male soldiers.

"Up to now," said a spokesman, "we have concentrated on recruiting transsexuals and women with small breasts.

"We now feel that the time is right to bring in men to serve in the army, despite the obvious objections to their presence in a modern fighting force."

But General Cynthia Surgical-Procedure, 56, 24, 32, was unconvinced. "Men have many traditional qualities," she said, "like an ability to cook, sew or be a vicar, but they would be out of place in the front line."

Those Regiments In Full

The Royal Army Transgender Corps
The Queen's Own Queens
The Blackwatch Undies
The Coldcream Guards
The Royal Corps of Confusing Signals
(That's enough regiments. Ed.).

IS THIS THE SON OF BIRT?

IN A sensational new £8 million landmark documentary series to be shown on Sundays throughout the Easter period, the BBC will take a radical new look at the most important and influential figure in world history – Greg Dyke.

Using the latest computer-imaging technology, experts have painstakingly assembled the most accurate image ever known of the man who, believers claim, is the saviour of the BBC.

Says Professor Botney, of the White City Institute for Men With Beards, "It is an extraordinary experience to find oneself confronted by this charismatic personality who altered the course of human civilisation by moving the news to 10 o'clock.

THE BIRT OF OUR LORD

"We can clearly see at last," he said, "a simple man who wandered about performing no miracles and who was crucified for losing snooker to Sky Sports 4. Truly, this man was the son of Birt."

What You Will Hear on BBC's Radio 4

(Chairman Sir Pigling Bland)

Brian Perkins *(for it is he)*: You have reached the BBC but the 8 O'clock News you wish to hear is not available.

If you wish to listen to Radio 3's composer of the week – Vivaldi's Four Seasons – press 3. If you wish to hear Terry Wogan playing Vivaldi's Four Seasons, press 2. If you wish to hear how much money Johnny Vaughan is being paid, press 5 followed by six noughts. If you wish to listen to the Today programme, please hold. The time sponsored by Accurist is 8.05.

John Humphrys: Thank you for holding. You've now reached the Today programme with John Humphrys and on the line I have the chairman of BT, Sir Pigling Bland.

Humphrys: Good morning, Sir Pigling.

Pigling: Good morning, John.

Humphrys: Could you speak up a bit, Sir Pigling, this line isn't very good.

Pigling: How dare you criticise me in my new job. You're fired.

Jim Naughtie *(for it is he)*: Sir Pigling, these new figures that BT is in debt to the tune of £30bn must be very... reassuring for you. What are your plans for the future of BT, Sir Pigling?

Pigling: Well, Jim, I intend to increase charges, hire a lot of consultants and sack most of the staff.

Naughtie: Bold stuff, Sir Pigling. And anything else?

Pigling: Well, obviously, Jim, I'm going to hire Johnny Vaughan to be the voice of the speaking clock so that we can win over more young listeners to dial up our time service.

Naughtie: This is tremendously exciting news, Sir Pigling. Of course, your critics might say that you are doing almost *too* well in your new job.

Pigling: Are you criticising me? You're fired.

Perkins: And now Thought For The Day with the new BT Chairman, His Holiness The Dalai Bland.

Bland: You know, a lot of people say to me, "Sir Pigling, I don't believe in BT any more, it's like the BBC, it just doesn't work in the modern world, but I always say to them, 'How dare you! You're fired!'"

(Cont. 94khz)

ROYAL NAVY 2000

"Now, now, Bo'sun, you know the rules – no public displays of affection!"

Vanishing Britain
With Magnus Drinklater

No. 94 Silence In The Glen

AS THE highland mist lies over the purple heather on the banks of Loch Nokia, the only sound is the plaintive wail of a lone piper, clad in his traditional garb of kilt and trainers.

He is playing an ancient lament to mark the ending of one of the oldest crafts in Scotland's proud history.

For hundreds of years, the guid folk of Bathgate have toiled in their crofts to produce the familiar single malt mobile phone, known the world over for its subtle blend of American technology and sheep droppings, distilled to a formula which has been handed down from father to son for well over two years.

"Aye, och, ye will nae see the like o' it again," mourned veteran assembler Jock McSimcard, as he looked sadly at the last NX747 which will ever come off the legendary Bathgate production line.

"'Tis a sad day, the noo," he wept, "tae see the end of the craft community of auld Motorola. Still, nae matter. The wee phones are nae fockin' use tae man nair beast. I'm awa' doon the chippie for ma tea."

THE Sun

Friday, May 24, 2001   30p

YES, HE'S GOING HOME

The Great Brain Robber

by Our Entire Staff

AT LAST, thanks to your No. 1 Sun, one of the world's most notorious villains has been put on a plane and sent back home to face the music, following a lifetime on the run, living off his ill-gotten gains.

Rupert Murdoch, who's somehow managed to avoid being collared by the world's tax inspectors, has been committing daylight robbery in almost every country he's visited over the last five decades. For years the old lag enjoyed the high life – if he wasn't cavorting with an exotic Asian beauty on the beach, he was entertaining the great and good in one of his many palatial residences.

But enough is enough – justice must prevail. Mr Murdoch must know it's time he was sent back to Australia to suffer the consequences of his many crimes, the worst of which must surely be flying Ronnie Biggs back to England in a disgraceful attempt to rip off the British taxpayer.

NO, HE'S NOT COMING HOME

by Our Entire Staff

JACK MILLS, the train driver involved in the Great Train Robbery, has stunned no one this week by not returning to Britain.

The Sun has attempted to entice him back home to Blighty from the Afterlife – a haven for people who've been coshed over the head by criminals – to no avail.

"He seems strangely reluctant to share a pint of beer in a pub in Margate or fish and chips on the pier with Ronnie Biggs, but we think he's holding out for money," said a bemused senior Sun *(cont. p. 94)*

THE Sun

Apology

In recent months, in common with all other right-wing newspapers, we may have given the mistaken impression that criminals are nothing more than scum with evil in their hearts, whose arrogant flouting of the law of the land means they deserve to be shot in the back rather than being lavished with free gifts and air travel endorsed by bleeding heart broadsheet press.

We now realise, in the light of us organising Ronnie Biggs's return to Britain, that criminals are in fact cheeky chappies with a song in their heart whose audacious flouting of the law of the land means they deserve a pat on the back and to be lavished with gifts of air travel and of £20,000 by your bleedin' brilliant super soaraway Sun.

We apologise for any confusion caused, and by any confusion caused in the future when we change our minds after the next young thug is rewarded with trainers and CDs, and we change it back again after we track down Lord Lucan.

PLUS: Dirty Old Digger Gets Young Asian Babe up the Duff! Hundreds of Sexy Pix!!

(cont. p. 94)

ROY of the FUGGERS

FUGHAM. F.C. ARE DIVISION ONE CHAMPIONS!

WE REPRESENT THE BEST IN ENGLISH FOOTBALL

YES, OUR TOP SCORER, MANAGER AND CHAIRMAN ARE ALL FOREIGN

FUGGIT!

LATE NEWS

Ronald Biggs's Sun breaks down in press conference

THE Sun newspaper today collapsed in an emotional heap of drivel at the news that no one cared about Ronnie Biggs.

Sobbing uncontrollably, the Sun, who had accompanied Ronnie Biggs from Rio and stayed at his side throughout the flight, said, "It's terrible. We're a sick newspaper. We're incoherent and mentally ill. All we wanted was a decent front page story. Now we find that the public want to lock us up and throw away the key."

TEACHERS STRIKE FALTERS

by our **Education Staff**

THE TEACHERS strike, which began at 9.30 this morning, ran into trouble by 3.30 in the afternoon when teachers insisted on going home early.

Said one, "I am not going to strike for more than 35 hours a week and to expect any further commitment from me is totally unreasonable." He continued, "People have no idea of the pressures on striking teachers. They think we just turn up on the picket line and start not working but we have to spend a lot of free time preparing the strike, getting the materials together, writing placards, photocopying leaflets and going down the pub for a staff meeting."

He then continued, "And what's more we have to cram in all this striking before the summer holidays. I mean it is outrageous" *(cont. p. 94)*

(cont. p. 94)

Metropolitan Police Notice

WANTED

Have you seen this man? He is believed to have been involved in a number of war crime incidents between the years 1990 and 1991 in the Baghdad area of Iraq. The police are very anxious to interview this gentleman, who may now be using the name 'Saddam Hussein' or 'Adolf Hitler'.

If you see this man, do not attempt to have a go, as he may be armed with weapons of mass-destruction, such as nuclear missiles, anthrax, nerve gas, etc, sufficient to destroy the entire human race. Members of the public are advised to leave the arrest of the wanted man to the Metropolitan Police, who already have a team of three highly-trained officers to deal with this situation in a pro-active manner – ie, flying off to Baghdad to apprehend the miscreant in his nuclear bunker with the words "Come along, Mr Hussein, sir, the game is up."

NEWS IN BRIEF

Fergie's former aide on murder rap   **2**

Di's former butler on teapot theft charge   **3**

Sophie's former partner in drugs row   **4**

Camilla's aunt's brother-in-law accused of damaging hotel trouser press   **5**

Someone who once met Princess Alexandra's daughter must pay parking fine   **6**

Country falls apart   **94**

Top stars send their kids to St Cakes

by Our Education Staff
Chris Bighead and **John Claire-de-Looney**

MORE and more parents are queueing up to get their children into the prestigious Black Country public school which is known as "the Eton of the West Midlands".

Among the showbiz legends who are hoping to enter their offspring to the £36,000-a-term boarding school of St Cakes are rock billionaire Mick Jagger and the world's highest-paid female singer Mrs Madonna Ritchie.

MATERIAL GIRLSCHOOL

The headmaster of St Cakes, Mr R.S.J. Kipling, told reporters yesterday "I cannot possibly comment on private and confidential entrance applications, but off-the-record I can tell you I am thrilled to think that Mick and Maddy, as they have asked me to call them, will soon be appearing at Prizegiving and making speeches about their latest records."

Said Mr Kipling, "We are also delighted to think that two such distinguished role models will be sending their cheques to St Cakes in the near future."

Could You Pass The St Cakes Entrance Exam?

Time Allowed: 3 Hours.

❶ How much do you think your parents are worth?
  a) £10 million
  b) £20 million
  c) £10 billion

❷ Will your parents be prepared to appear in the School Prospectus?
Yes/No

❸ Would your parents like to sponsor our new Music School, the St Cakes Rock 'n' Roll Academy, and be prepared to star in a fund-raising concert for the new headmaster's house?
Yes/No

If all answers are satisfactory, candidates will be admitted to the school at once.

"Your school results are a disgrace – even for a boy"

de la Nougerede

Those Italian Election Results in Full

Mussolini North
Silvio Sleazoni *(Vota Formi)* 746,378 lira; Don Corleoni Mafiosi *(Cosa Nostra Democratic Christian alliance)* 878,442 lira; Luigi Corruptione *(Payola Scandale Party)*

1,756,437 lira; Captain Corelli *(Mandolini Party)* 0 votes.

Berlusconi gain by 6 channels

LATE NEWS
Berlusconi faces new charges

63

'PATHETIC LITTLE CREATURE' TO BE SPARED

by Our Political Staff **Simon Heiffer**

AFTER BEING buried alive under the foot and mouth epidemic for two months, farmers were amazed to find that little Tony the Prime Minister was still alive.

CALF-BAKED

"It's a miracle," said one. "You would have thought he would be dead and buried by now, but, amazingly, he is still alive."

There were still fears last week that he would have to be put down anyway, but instead the public have adopted him and taken him to their hearts.

MOO LABOUR

"Tony is so lovable and cute and sweet," said one eight-year-old fan

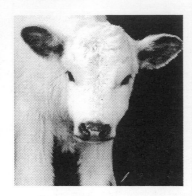

(Alastair Campbell). "He is perfectly healthy and it would be a tragedy if he were to be killed off just because he has been linked to a national disaster."

Phoenix is £4.99 per pound.

DANDO MAN 'DEFINITELY GUILTY'

by Our Crime Staff **E. Dunnit**

THE PROSECUTION in the Dando murder trial today produced the final conclusive piece of evidence which will nail Britain's most hated killer to the tragic death of the most popular TV personality in history.

The courtroom hushed as the jury were asked to "look very closely indeed" at a tiny particle of household dust, barely one-billionth of a millimetre long.

PARTICLE OF FAITH

"It is on this microspeck of domestic detritus," said Inspector 'Knacker of the Yard' Knacker, "that the whole of our case against the killer rests."

The court then heard evidence from forensic experts that the piece of dust found on the sole of the accused's shoe was "of exactly the same type, more or less" as dust found on a pavement close to the murdered TV star's West London home.

"I think you will agree," the inspector told the jury, "that finding this key piece of dust is as good as putting a noose around the guilty man's neck."

DUST PROOF

The press gallery, packed with fearless and unbiased investigative reporters, burst into spontaneous applause as the journalists began tapping into their laptops headlines such as "DANDO MAN 'DEFINITELY GUILTY'". *(To be continued.)*

Gardener's Tips No. 94

If you want your garden digging up for Spring, **writes Old Bore**, but can't do it yourself, simply ring up the police with "a new clue to the Lamplugh Mystery" and before you can say "waste of police time" hundreds of uniformed men will be turning over your garden.

© *Old Bore.*

Disposal of Pounds Criticised

THERE have been growing complaints about the economic impact of the Government decision to transport over a million healthy pounds every month, and dumping them into an enormous money pit in Greenwich.

"It's vital we dispose of the pounds in this way," said a Government spokesman, "because all the advice we're getting tells us this will provide a smokescreen and prevent the spread of articles about our inability to sell the Dome."

Despite Government assurances that this enormous money-pit won't cause any long-lasting suffering, many people living near the Dome have complained of feeling sick to the stomach, watching endless amounts of public money going up in smoke.

More Police Shock

THE Government today welcomed a 77% increase in the numbers of policemen on BBC television.

"Under the Conservatives we just had to make do with 'Dalziel and Pascoe' and 'Between the Lines'," said a clearly delighted Jack Straw, "but as a direct result of New Labour's initiatives, the number of fictional policemen on television has rocketed, with endless troubled detectives pounding the schedules.

"These extra policemen on the screen mean that people throughout Britain feel safe to stay in their homes at night."

Capitalism Demo

THE Government today urged the public to be on their guard against vicious mobs of capitalists that have been specially trained in America to wreak havoc.

At a given signal of economic slowdown these capitalists give a demonstration of their flagrant disregard for the pleas of Governments everywhere.

"They wish to 'smash the state' of British industry and they lash out at the first sign of a profits warning," said one concerned Anarchist. "Make no mistake – these hardcore capitalists are highly organised and behave as if they're a law unto themselves."

Reuters

"I've sold the exclusive rights to Van Eyck"

I-SPY

Thailand

NO DIVING

USA

B.U.M. EQUIPMENT

AGE Concern

INFORMATION SHOP →

Walding & Son

FUNERAL DIRECTORS

Uxbridge, Middlesex

BY APPOINTMENT TO
H R H THE PRINCE OF WALES
SUPPLIERS OF EXOTIC MUSHROOMS
McPHERSONS ATLANTIC LTD
PITLOCHRY

Pitlochry, Scotland

My Dung Restaurant

PECIALITIES .NINH HOA SPRING ROLL
.HOT SPOT SOUP

Vietnam

BADHOJEL

Black Forest

67 School of Nursing and Midwifery

Deliveries at rear of building

Southampton

Beware of the Elderly

Llandrindod Wells

Courier

TEACHER OF THE YEAR

-LATTEST NOMINATIONS-

Courier

BP

VISCO lubricants

Unleaded F·U·C
Lead free Four Star O·F·F
greener Diesel nO·8

London N11

HOTEL NEANDERTHAL

Italy

When Fire Alarm Sounds All Escape Windows must be Closed

Royal Dundee Liff Hospital

Tunbridge Wells, Kent

HOTEL COQ HARDI

Lille, France

SPECIAL OFFER

FRISKIES CANNED DOG
850
666g

2.15

Singapore supermarket

P WONG WAY

New Zealand

Barnes Hall N-V
Oedipus Complex ↑
Barnes Launderette ↑
No Parking
Emergency Vehicle Access
← Car Park A
CCTV SURVEILLANCE 24hr monit...

Keele University

a Camera
sic Room, Oxford

What next for the Tories?

Lord Jeffrey Archer

POSTPONED TO A LATER DATE

Trinity
All Members of the University Welcome

Trinity College, Oxford

Paradise
(No caravans or camping)

Lincolnshire

Turkey

yağınızı şimdi kontrol edin!..
BP Super V
yıllarca/güvenle

** CAUTION **
To avoid excessive splashing,
ALL TURDS
over 1.5kgs
must be lowered by hand.

Raratongan Hotel, Cook Islands

THE EYE'S TOP TEAM — BRINGING YOU THE MOST COMPREHENSIVE ELECTION COVERAGE EVER

FROM TODAY Private Eye will be running an extra 94 pages every issue to guarantee up-to-the-minute round-the-clock first-past-the-post in-depth behind-the-scenes in-your-face cut-out-and-throw-away reportage of tomorrow's events today.

This is the A-team who will deliver the nation's most indispensable election news before it even happens.

Man with glasses. With over 40 years' experience at the cutting edge, the man with glasses will provide analysis and comment.

Woman you haven't heard of. Reporting from the key marginals, the woman you haven't heard of will write thousands of words about the ups and downs of the campaign trail.

Young bloke. With no experience at all, young bloke will be giving a unique Generation X viewpoint on the issues that concern first-time voters.

Man with bowtie. One of Britain's top psephologists, man with bowtie will be conducting a daily poll of polls to keep you abreast of all the latest percentages.

Someone amusing. With his unique brand of wry humour, someone amusing will be taking a wry sideways look at the lighter moments of the election battle.

Another woman. To make the team look bigger and more balanced in gender terms, another woman will be getting a picture byline as well.

Alastair Campbell. Top government spokesman Alastair Campbell will be coming up with our stories, writing our headlines and telling us what to put in the editorials *(some mistake surely).*

More Top Team tomorrow

ADVERTISEMENT
WE HAVEN'T THROWN £63 MILLION OF YOUR MONEY AWAY

ADVERTISEMENT
LABOUR IS NOT WASTING MONEY ON ADVERTISING

ADVERTISEMENT
HOW DARE THE TORIES ACCUSE US OF EXPENSIVE PROPAGANDA?

RGJ

Do you know you haven't got any policies?

You hum it and I'll pick it up

THAT LABOUR ELECTION-WINNING STRATEGY IN FULL

1. Call the Election.
2. Remind everyone that William Hague is leader of the Conservative Party.
3. Er... that's it.

THE NEWS

(as seen and heard on all media)

Newsreader: Today the political parties will be concentrating on the environment and transport. The Lib Dem spokesman, Mr Sandy Beard, will visit a recycling plant in Truro. The Conservative spokesman Mr Sebastian Pinstripe will go on a walkabout near a proposed cycle lane in Croydon .And the Labour spokesman will unveil new plans to target toxic emissions from domestic barbecues.

And now the other news... Oldham is still on fire after the seventh successive night of rioting. Racial violence also spread to Aylesbury, where Asians and skinheads clashed. In Portadown in Northern Ireland, there were clashes between police and protestors – but let's forget all that and get back to the election.

Today it's your chance to put your questions on the environment and transport to the deputy spokesman of the Green Party, Simon Weed.

Caller: I live in Oldham and someone has just burned my house down. What are you going to do?

Weed: The Green Party has always made it clear that we are worried by the gases emitted by burning houses. That is why we fully support the Kyoto initiative which the European Parliament has ratified under Section...

Newsreader: I'm sorry, we've just had an urgent news flash that the Government Environment Secretary Mrs Voda Phone will be delivering a speech later today in which she will say that Labour are going to appoint a "Wheelie-Bin Czar" to crack down on overflowing wheelie bins.

We understand that the Conservative spokesman, Mr Jeremy Winebar, will attack the Wheelie-Bin Czar idea and claim that this initiative which would cost the country £20 billion, put £10 on the price of a gallon of petrol and permit Brussels to allow millions of asylum seekers to live in the front room of your burning house *(continued on all channels until 7 June)*

PARLIAMENTARY DEBATES

(Han-z-z-z-ard)

Final Session of Parliament Before Government Returns For Second Term

3.17pm
Prime Minister's Questions

Patsy Jacket (Waitrose East, Lab): Does Tony, I mean the Prime Minister, sorry Tony, do you agree that you have done so spectacularly well in the last four years that there's really no need to have another election ever again?

(Labour cheers)

Rt. Hon. Tony Blair: Well, Patsy, er, I really think it's important not to get too complacent about this. I mean, I know we're going to win, but some of the public might like to feel that they are part of the process, and I think that's very important.

Karen Laptop (Tesco North, Lab): Could I just say how much I agree with Patsy, and that it's wonderful that everyone's got another chance to show how much they love Tony and support everything he's doing?

Tony Blair *(reading from notes)*: I would like to point out that, in real terms, the percentage increase in fundholding support initiatives across the regions has risen by 56 percent, which is 27 percent more than anything achieved by the party opposite during their 18 years of sleaze, incompetence and boom-and-bust.

(Tories cries of "Answer! Answer!")

The Speaker (Hon. Jimmy Gorbals MP): Order, order, order the noo!

Blair: Thank you, Mr Speaker, for that eloquent and helpful contribution. I'm so glad I gave you the job.

Speaker: The Rt. Hon. Leader of the Opposition, Wee Wullie Hague.

William Hague (Boddington, Con): Would the Prime Minister not agree that he's been not so much running the country for the last four years, but ruining it?

(Tory laughter and cheers)

Furthermore, Mr Speaker, would it not be true to say that the Prime Minister's record is so bad that it would sell fewer copies than one by Miss Geri Halliwell?

(Hysterical laughter from Tory Benches, except Mr Portillo. Cries from older members of "Who is Geri Halliwell?")

It's the way I tell 'em! And here's another one! This bloke goes into a pub and says, "14 pints of best Yorkshire ale, please." And the barman says, "You look as if you've had enough." And the man says, "You're right there, I've had enough of Tony Blair – which is why I need to drink so much!"

(Tories pass out in paroxysms of unstoppable mirth)

Mr Blair: I don't know how the Rt. Hon. gentleman has got the nerve to stand there cracking jokes when his government was responsible for 18 years of sleaze, incompetence and boom-and-bust.

Mr Hague: Would the prime minister agree that his letters to the Hinduja brothers...

Mr Speaker: You shut your face, laddie. We dinnae want that sort of talk in here. I now call on the Rt. Hon. Edward Heath, the Father of the House, to reminisce for several hours about his 51 years as an ornament of this House.

Rt. Hon. Edward Heath (Beijing, Con): Hullo. I am delighted to see so many of you have come along to pay your respects to the greatest parliamentarian of this or any other generation. Namely myself. Not since the days of Pitt the Grocer has there been a more redoubtable champion of the rights of this chamber, which is why I thought it was only right to give away its powers to the unelected Commission in Brussels. I am sure that history will recognise that I was right, and that all my successors were completely wrong, on this and all other matters. I will not deign to mention the name of Mrs Thatcher, the most disastrous prime minister of all time. And while I am about it, as a loyal Conservative, I would like to say that I hope no one will be foolish enough to vote for this pathetic little right-wing extremist who is now passing himself off as the leader of a party which was once in happier times fortunate enough to be led by such eminent statesmen as myself.

(Cries from Tories of "Bring back Maggie!" "Bring back Major!", "Bring back anyone!")

Speaker: Are there any other Members who would like to offer a wee word or twa afore they gang?

Rt. Hon. Tony Benn (Teabag, Lab): Mishta Shpeaker, itsh not only my very good friend Ted who feels utterly betrayed by his Party. I would jusht like to shay how much I hate everything that thish New Labour government standsh for, and as for Mr Blair...

Speaker: That's quite enough from you too, laddie. Yer time's up.

Mr Paddy Ashtray (Pantsdown, Lib Dem): Since I am also leaving this House, may I just take this opportunity to attack Charles Kennedy. He must be the worst leader of the Lib Dems since the last one, whose name everyone has forgotten...

(House empties as MPs try to remember where their constituencies are)

IT'S **VAZ**

BRITAIN'S TOP COMIC!

I'VE BEEN FORCED TO SIT OUT THE ELECTION DUE TO ILL HEALTH AND EXHAUSTION...

DON'T GET WELL SOON

EVERYONE'S _SICK_ AND _TIRED_ OF ME!!

PASS PORT CASH

SPIN DOCTOR

ONLY KIDDING READERS!!

... RGJ

IN TODAY's 94-page election special, we bring you all the pieces you don't want to read, by the Eye's top team.

Man with glasses analyses the Brown-Blair rift. Could the national insurance ceiling issue prove the straw that breaks the Chancellor's back? p. 3

Woman you haven't heard of joins the Lib Dem battlebus on the M29 to Skegness. A surprisingly bouncy Charles

Kennedy is confident that his "penny on income tax" pledge will woo the floating "grey vote" – or will it? p. 5

Young bloke visits an inner city primary school in Solihull and asks the kids whether they've heared of Francis Maude. A surprising 0 percent say "yes". p. 6

Man with bowtie conducts a "poll of polls" and concludes that Labour could well win this election. p. 7

Someone amusing accompanies Ann Widdecombe

in the Widdiecopter and notices that she's quite fat and has a squeaky voice. p. 11

Another woman looks at the media coverage of the election and asks "Is there an anti-woman bias in media election teams?" p. 15

Old man bemoans the lack of excitement in modern elections, and remember how different things were in the old days. p. 17

PLUS Cartoonist of the Year **Martin Bummer** takes a wry sideways look at John Prescott, and asks "Is he New Labour's answer to Lennox Lewis?"

PLUS Domestic supergoddess **Nigella Lawson** unveils her easy-to-cook "election night al fresco supper for six".

RECIPE

1. Phone up Pizza Hut.
2. Tell Darren where you live.
3. Ask for six deep-pan thick-crust American Hots with extra cheese.
4. Answer door.
5. Receive plaudits from guests.
6. Put in new book.
7. Receive large cheque from publisher.

© Nigella Sound-Bites 2001.

BLAIR BLAMES TELEVISION FOR 'ELECTION STUNTS'

by Our Political Staff **Andrew Marrvelous**

TONY BLAIR lashed out last night at television companies who are trying to undermine Labour's campaign by "filming cheap stunts" rather than concentrating on the real issues.

The Prime Minister spoke out during a spontaneous visit to an old people's home where he had tea with a toddler before meeting some disabled pets. He said, "It is disgraceful that television reporters persistently film embarrassing moments such as this one which have been deliberately set up as photo opportunities."

Removing his jacket and pausing only to sing the first two verses of the hymn 'All things bright can only get better,' he continued, "How dare the media try to manipulate this election for the sake of a few pictures on the evening news? That is my job."

Tony Blair is 47% ahead of William Hague for some reason.

Yes, you sir – the man who has been planted to ask me an easy question

---

Daily Mail

Economic Meltdown Imminent

THIS newspaper can exclusively reveal that the economy might perhaps be slightly slowing down a bit.

This is catastrophic news for Labour, as it will surely mean that in the next twelve months we'll see house prices plummet, unemployment soar, the pound collapse, Britain plunged back into a primitive feudal system, giant lizards roaming the Earth and the Conservative Party being returned to power.

● **Full story inside editor's imagination.**

HOW I WILL VOTE

by DR ADAM HEARTTHROB from the top medical soap ENT (played by actor Robson Jerome – real name Jerome Robson)

WE'RE RIGHT in the middle of filming episode 797 of the new ENT series but if I do get out to vote I think I'll probably vote Lib Dem or possibly Green. My Dad was a Tory, which means I might swing that way but I think Tony Blair has done a good job and we should give him a second chance.

TOMORROW: Brooklyn Beckham puts the case for voting UKIP.

The Mirror, *Friday, June 15, 2001*

PANTS!

By Our Political Staff CALVIN KLEIN

YES! It's the question everyone in politics wants to know. What sort of pants does Piers Morgan wear? Now it can be revealed. They're brown!

Says Piers, "Of course they are brown. But it's nothing to do with fashion. It's because I'm terrified of being sacked and going to jail after the DTI investigation into my dodgy share dealings.

"That's why," he continued, "my newspaper says Vote Labour! The Government is wonderful! Blair is marvellous! Give me, I mean Tony, another chance."

Daily Mail

Lady Thatcher Speaks Exclusively To The Mail's Simon Heffalump

SHE shimmered into the room, a vision in blue, looking not a day older than her 436 years. I was reminded of Shakespeare's immortal tribute to her all those years ago: "Age cannot wither her, nor the years forget".

"How are you, Prime Minister?" I tentatively enquired, with a lump in my throat as I contemplated her infinite loveliness.

"I can't wait to get back to Number Ten and sort out that ghastly little man, Major," she told me, her voice rising to a crescendo of passion and burning love for her country.

"Has anyone ever told me you look beautiful when you're angry?" I asked her, as I knelt *(cont'd. p. 94)*

THAT LIB DEM MANIFESTO IN FULL

1. Admit they're going to raise taxes to deliver improved public services.
2. Don't get elected.
3. Er... that's it...

THAT TORY MANIFESTO IN FULL

1. Claim they're going to cut taxes to deliver improved public services.
2. Don't get elected.
3. Er... that's it...

THAT LABOUR MANIFESTO IN FULL

1. Get elected.
2. Er... that's it...

HAGUE FEVER BRINGS MISERY TO MILLIONS

by Our Medical Staff **Ann T. Histamine**

MILLIONS of Britons were warned today to stay indoors for the next two weeks, particularly on 7 June when forecasters predict the highest levels of Hague Fever on record.

Said a doctor: "What happens is that Hague gets up the patient's nose, and they begin to feel irritation or possibly drowsiness. It is important that sufferers do not do anything mechanical, such as vote or drive to a polling station, whilst experiencing the symptoms of Hague Fever."

Opinion Pollen

However, relief is at hand because experts predict that by the end of June Hague Fever will disappear for ever, to be replaced by Spanish Flu (or *Portillosis desperatis,* to give it the full medical term).

To read more about Hague Fever, visit our website www.achoo.co.uk where you will find details of our helpline (0908 7643278), which will tell you where to buy this magazine.

SEVEN DAYS TO SAVE THE HAGUE

"Not another bloody repeat"

LABOUR ELECTION LANDSLIDE

Election Results In Full

Middle England Central

Mike Lobbyfodder (Lab) 22,374; Libby Dem (Lib Dem) 19,748; Nicholas Washedup (Conservative) 3,722: Sandra Swampy (Green) 278; Dave Scargs (Socialist Alliance) 3; CJP Barking (UKIP) 3

Swing .01% to Labour

CHARLES KENNEDY
An Apology

IN COMMON with all other newspapers, we may have given the impression that the leader of the Liberal Democrat Party Mr Charles Kennedy was in some way a political lightweight, a joke figure, and a "chat show Charlie", who could never be taken seriously by the electorate and whose party therefore faced wipe-out in the recent election. We may further have given the impression that, in comparison, his predecessor Lord Pantsdown of Sarajevo was a towering giant bestriding the political scene like a colossus. Headlines such as "Ginger Your Nuts", "Calamity Kennedy Heads Lib Dems For Meltdown" and "Is Lib Dem Chazza Drunk and Gay? – We Do Hope So" may have conveyed to readers the idea that we were in some way critical of Mr Kennedy's abilities.

In the light of the election results, we now recognise that there was not a jot or a scintilla of truth in any of the above, and would like to make it clear that Mr Kennedy is one of the most outstanding political leaders of this or any other century, a master strategist and spellbinding orator of unequalled personal charisma, who is the greatest Liberal statesman since Lord Jenkins of Hillhead *(Surely Gladstone? Ed.)*. We hope that today's headlines, such as "It's Skye-High Charlie!", "Sex-Bomb Kennedy Is The Ladies' Favourite" and "Why Is Goodtime Chazza Not At Number Ten Instead of Boring, Teetotal Blair?" will correct our earlier misleading innuendoes and apologise for any confusion caused.

"They've romped into third place"

LIB DEM TRIUMPH

You were a good loser, William

Yes – I was brilliant

WHO WILL BE THE NEW CAPTAIN OF THE TITANIC?

By Our Political Staff **Michael Whitestarline**

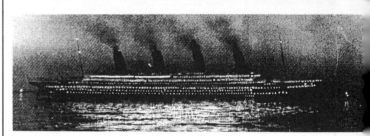

WILLIAM Hague has sensationally quit his post as Captain of the Titanic after the second sinking of the vessel in only four years.

At the weekend, a number of hopefuls were already throwing their caps into the icy water.

First to declare herself was the ship's matron, Miss Doris Karloff, who has been described by experts as "unthinkable". She said last night:

"William has done a superb job in sinking the boat with the loss of all hands. But now it really is time for someone else to steer us into the iceberg again.

"I shall be glug glug glug," she told reporters.

Various other members of the crew were also keen to take command of the bridge, foremost amongst them the Spanish-born purser Michael Porthole, who has already teamed up with former first officer Kenneth Clark.

ANCRAM'S AWAY

"Together we could really go places," said Porthole enthusiastically, "like the bottom of the ocean. Glug... glug... glug."

Others who have put their name forward for the merchant navy's top job are:

● **Ian Suncan-Smith, described as an intensely able swimmer.**

● **Tim Yeo - Must - Be - Joking** known to be very much at home in a life jacket.

● **Francis Overbaude, a man who many believe will effectively take the ship all the way to Drowning Street.** *(That's enough Titanic story. Ed.)*

Margaret Cook

Dear Margaret

Over the past decade I've enjoyed a committed, long-term relationship with a man called Tony. He's always been very good to me and I thought we had something special, then out of the blue the other day he dumped me for Jack. Now I find out from Gordon that he's been plotting behind my back to get rid of me for months. To be so casually tossed aside in such a brutal callous manner after years of faithful service is devastating. I feel angry, bitter, resentful and yet curiously powerless. Tony's even told me to return the keys of my precious country house. What do you think of the callous brutal way I've been treated?
Robin
(address supplied – London)

Dear Robin

Ha ha ha ha ha ha.
Margaret

DAILY MAIL-CHAUVINIST EXCLUSIVE

WIDDECOMBE'S AMAZING MAKEOVER

BEFORE: hard, tough, uncompromising

AFTER: caring, sharing, electable

"Great evening – what a low turn-out!"

OLD BAGS (SURELY 'GAGS'?) REVISITED

Do you know who I am?

Ask the Matron, dear. She'll tell you...

Never Too Old...

by Sylvie Krin

THE STORY SO FAR:
Billionaire media mogul Rupert Murdoch has married the willowy almond-eyed prawn cracker of the East, Wendy Deng, but his children from the first Mrs Murdoch have always looked down on the amber goddess from the land of pot noodles.
Now read on...

IT was 4 o'clock in the morning as a summer dawn broke over the Manhattan skyline. On the 94th floor of the Perry Como building an old man shuffled reluctantly from his bedroom to a Redgrave and Pinsent Olmpic standard rowing machine, an 87th birthday present from his fragrant oriental wifette.

"I've set it for 3 hours uphill rapids," she cooed lovingly from her boudoir three floors away. "Chop, chop, Lupert. I'll come and see you later if you're still alive. Just joking, ha ha ha!"

The morning seemed to last an eternity as the proud tycoon struggled to put on his designer tracksuit and began his punishing daily regime. As the hours ticked slowly away, he cast his mind back to that rare night of passion in September when, for a few fleeting moments, Wendy had made him feel a young man again.

Just like all those years ago in the outback when he rode a kangaroo from the sheep station at Diggery Doo to old Rolf's Abbo's Armpit Club in dusty Alice Thompson. Happy days then when, as a virile, carefree young jackaroo he had wanged his donger and watched the Sheilas' eyes pop with pleasure...

"Lupert! What you do dreaming? No slacking!" The shrill voice of the sultry beauty from Beijing interrupted his reverie as she hit him playfully with a copy of the New South Wales Courier and Argus.

"Look! It says here I have bun in oven. What this mean?"

"Well, darling," wheezed the global media magnate, as the perspiration poured down his wrinkled cheeks, "it means that when you cough out the little feller, he gets a big slice of his daddy's dosheroo."

"I don't get it, Lupert," she cried.

"That's right, my little fortune-hunting cookie," he spluttered. "The little bugger gets all the money. Mind you, I'd have to croak first."

Wendy's beautiful eyes narrowed inscrutably and her hand moved to the setting on the rowing machine marked "Dangerous. Not suitable for rich old men."

(To be continued...)

PEARL HARBOR BOMBS

by Our Film Staff Jonathan Dross

"WE DIDN'T see the attacks coming," said the producers of the film Pearl Harbor. **"The assaults were unprovoked and cowardly and we were** sitting ducks. We had no chance to defend ourselves as wave upon wave of hostile critics blew our film out of the water."

Said Disney spokesman, Mr Michael J. Mouse III, "We thought a huge American film like this was indestructible. With its state-of-the-art technology and billion dollar fire power, we thought it was guaranteed to be safe."

BORA! BORA! BORA!

He continued, "Unfortunately, the enemy reviewers identified a weakness in our defences. The film is no bloody good. And they showed no mercy. We're going down the Kami Khazi."

Daily Mail

Friday, June 1, 2001 — Newspaper of the Year 35p

Is The Bikini Coming Back?
Hundreds of pics of birds in bikinis

Can This Superbra Give You A 46 D-Cup over night?
More pics of girls in bras

Why Does Channel Five Keep On Pumping Out Soft Porn Every Night?
More pics of girls not even wearing bras

A Taxi-Driver Writes A Novel

*THIS WEEK Private Eye begins an exclusive eight-week serialisation of the new novel "Blimey Guv" by **Richard Littlejohn** (voted Britain's Number One Cabbie by Cabs & Cabmen Magazine, 1997)*

Chapter One
Blimey Guv! What's this country coming to? I mean to say!

Chapter Two
These asylum seekers, for example. If I had my way I'd string 'em all up!

Chapter Three
It's the only language they understand!

Chapter Four
Except they *don't,* cos none of them can speak the Queen's English! Right guv?!?

Chapter Five
Wanna go over Kew Bridge or Tower Bridge to Heathrow, Guv? Either way the traffic's murder! I blame the social workers and the Guardian readers and the do-gooders myself.

Chapter Six
Get out of the f***ing way! Bloody cyclists! They should be strung up an' all!

Chapter Seven
I had a bloke from HarperCollins in the back once! A real gentleman! He gave me hundreds of thousands of pounds to write a book!?! Blimey Guv – I mean, what's the country coming to?!

© World copyright Richard Littlebrain

New Book's Shock Claim

CHARLES AND PHILIP 'DON'T GET ON'

By Our Royal Correspondent
Richard Kaygiarist

A SENSATIONAL new account of the life of the Duke of Edinburgh reveals that the 80-year-old Duke does not always "see eye-to-eye" with his son Charles, 52.

The author of these shock revelations, which throw an entirely new light on the personal relationship between the Queen's husband and her son, is believed to have read over 100,000 old press cuttings before reaching his devastating conclusions.

PHIL THE PAGE

Among the astonishing claims made in an article in the Daily Telegraph, which I read yesterday, are that:

● Prince Philip packed his son off to a boarding school rather than have him at home

● Prince Philip forced his son into the Navy, when Charles wanted to become a ballerina

● The Duke strongly disapproved of all his son's girlfriends, including Diana and Camilla, and told him to "get a grip"

● The Duke is an incredible 80-year-old, but tries to keep this a secret.

For Full Story Read Yesterday's Daily Telegraph
(Surely pages 18-36? P.D.)

THAT PRINCE PHILIP LETTER TO PRINCE CHARLES IN FULL

TOP SECRET & CONFIDENTIAL

BALMORAL

Tuesday

Dear Sir,
It has been brought to my attention that in a recent book it has been claimed that I am "distant, cold, remote and stand-offish with regard to Prince Charles". That is why I have asked my secretary to write this letter to you expressing my deep regret that untrue sentiments should have ever been attributed to myself.

Commander Sir Percival
Goodtrouser (RN Retd)
pp HRH Duke of Edinburgh

P.S. Grow up you big girl's blouse and STOP blubbering!

"You couldn't pick it up"

72

A Twist In The Tale

by Jeffrey Archer

THE STORY SO FAR: Master storyteller Godfrey Bowman is facing trial on a trumped up charge of perjury.

Only days before he is due in the dock, a vital witness, Malrika Coughdrop, dies in a mysterious hit-and-run incident.

Now read on...

"**M**ay I ask you, Mr Bowman, where you were on the night of the 27th of April when this poor lady met her death?"

The 47-year-old Chief Inspector looked menacingly at the tanned, fit, handsome, physically active former brain surgeon turned novelist.

"That's easy, Inspector," he replied, quickly filling in his diary for the night in question. "Look, it says here that I was having dinner at the Caprice with a young slapper."

The Chief Inspector raised a quizzical eyebrow at the former astronaut and world heavyweight champion.

"And what would be the name of the slapper in question?"

"I think her name was Sally, now that you mention it," trilled Bowman's fragrant wife, Mandy, the world-famous nuclear scientist, who had unexpectedly entered the room following a photoshoot on the front lawn for members of the tabloid press.

"Thank you, ma'am," said the Chief Inspector, scribbling dutifully in his notebook. "But what makes you think I will believe any of this?"

Bowman silently handed over a brown envelope to the policeman. "Perhaps you should leave the country at this juncture?" he said pointedly, winking conspiratorially.

But then there was a twist in the tale. An amazing development in the story which no one had thought of.

Bowman was innocent. He had nothing to do with it at all. "I just don't believe it!" said everyone.

© J. Archer (based on a story by someone else and written by Richard Cohen)

CHARLES IN CANADA

How do they call you, white man?

Big Chief Never-Going-To-Be-King

THE BOOK OF AMIEL

Chapter 94

1. And behold, there was a woman of Is-rael whose name was Bar-bara, daughter of Amiel.

2. And she was exceeding comely, even as are the maidens who adorn the sea coast of Eilat in the posters that offereth a cheap winter break.

3. And, lo, there was a certain rich man, who was called Con-rad. And he espied Bar-bara and said unto himself, "I would lie with her, for she is truly an dish".

4. Then Con-rad put aside his wife and took unto himself Bar-bara, and they lived together as man and wife in the wharf that is called Can-ary.

5. And Bar-bara cometh unto her husband and saith "Behold, I am filled with prophecy. I see my people Is-rael sorely beset on every hand".

6. "For the Arab-ites and the Araf-ites have risen up against them, and cast stones upon them. And the children of Is-rael have nothing with which to defend themselves, excepts tanks, planes, rockets and attack helicopters."

7. And Con-rad saith unto her "What shall I do?"

8. And she spelleth it out "Give me an whole page of your newspaper, which is called the Daily Telaviv (*Surely 'graph'? God*), that I may fill it with my prophetic utterances – ie, that the children of Is-rael must keep smiting, for it is the only language these Arab-ites understand."

9. And Con-rad did as he was commanded, because he was sore afraid of his wife.

10. And so it came to pass that the prophet Amiel was able to speak out with a loud voice on behalf of the children of Is-rael.

11. And Sharon, the ruler of the land of Is-rael, rejoiced exceeding glad, saying "Look, not everyone thinketh that I am a bully and a monger of wars. For here is a mighty prophetess who agreeth with everything I have done, except that when it cometh to the smiting, she wanteth even more of it."

Radio 4
The Today Programme

What You Missed...

Jim Naughtiebutdim *(for it is he)*: ...and later this morning Libby Purves's guests on Midweek will be the man who invented a squirrel-proof birdfeeder, the author of a new book about Sibelius's piano music, an ex-nun who spent six years in the Foreign Legion and a wine grower from the Hebrides.

But now, the Today programme has the honour and privilege to celebrate the birthday of perhaps the greatest singer, songwriter, composer and poet of all time, Bob Dylan.

And first, we're very fortunate to have someone in the studio, Reg Nargs of the legendary Sixties' group Green Gerbil, who is going to recreate one of Dylan's greatest masterpieces.

Nargs *(Strum, strum, strummity-strum. Sings)*: Hey, man, whereya goin'/You ain't gonna get very far/Cos you ain't gotta Cadillac car... *(Strum, strummily-strum.)*

Naughtie *(weeping with pleasure)*: That was frankly incredible to think that one man could not only write those unforgettable lyrics, but the music to go with them. But now, we have an even greater privilege, the chance of a word with one of the greatest musical geniuses of this or any other time. I am, of course, referring to that legendary figure Blind Lemon Shandy

Levine. Are you there, Blind Lemon?

Levine: Sho, man, where am I? I am where I am, 'cos I am where I is.

Naughtie: That's just amazing. To think that we were listening there to the actual voice of Blind Lemon Shandy Levine. And now, on this historic day, when everyone in the world will be thinking of Bob Dylan, one can only say that it is a privilege and an honour to utter his name here on the Today programme. And so, to conclude our homage, to the uncrowned all-time king of popular music, back now to Reg Nays, who will recreate the title song from Bob Dylan's immortal album "I'm Going No Place".

Nargs *(Strum, strummity, strum, strum. Sings)*: I'm a-goin' no place/'Cos that's the place I'm goin' to... *(Strummity, strummity, strum.)*

J. Humphrys *(for it is now he)*: Incredible! What a privilege to have that unforgettable song played right here in the Today Studio. And now, Though For The Day, with Rabbi Ahmed Bajanda Fotherington-Smythe, of the United Reformed Synagogue of Tibet.

Rabbi: You know, when I was watching the Liberal Democrats' election broadcast last night, I turned to my partner and said *(Cont. 94 Mhz)*

"You have to be really well organised to be an anarchist"

The Lion, The Witch And The Wardrobe Full Of Gold

by C.S. Lewis (newly adapted for the 21st Century)

holden after Baynes

In this exciting new adventure story, Harper and Collins are staying at their rich Uncle Murdoch's house, when they discover a mysterious wardrobe. When they open it, imagine their surprise when they find inside a pile of dusty old books.

When they show them to their uncle, he tells them that the books can be magically turned into a huge pile of gold. All they have to do is to take out all the boring Christian bits (ie, plot, characters, story) and rewrite them themselves in the style of the great Sir Walter Disney. Harper and Collins set about their task with relish, and within a few months they have become the richest people in the world (or rather Uncle Murdoch has). And so winter returned to Narnia for ever.

Today – Only In Private Eye
THE TOP 100 MOST BORING LISTS IN BRITAIN
Compiled by Phil Supplement

1 **The *Sunday Times* Rich List** *(Last year's position – 1)*

INCREDIBLY dull list of boring people with pictures of the Queen and Paul McCartney to try and persuade you that it isn't as boring as it looks.

2 **The *Sunday Times* Young Rich List**

NEWCOMER in the Boring Top Hundred, this list is not quite as dull as the full Rich List, but is considerably duller than the Rich Asian List, the Rich Dotcom List, the Young Rich Asian Dotcom List and *(That's enough boring lists. Ed.)*

BILLIE
IS SHE OR ISN'T SHE?
The Question The Whole Nation Is Asking

IT's the question that the whole nation is asking. *(You've done this in the headline, you idiot. Ed.)* Is she or isn't she? Some are convinced that she is. But others are sure that she isn't. It's the question that the whole nation is asking. *(Get on with it or you're fired. Ed.)*

Is teen singing sensation Billie mad? The tell-tale signs are clear for everyone to see:

1. **She has married Chris Evans.**
2. **Er…**
3. **That's it.**

THE SUN SAYS

She's mad – and so are we to run this drivel.

CATHERINE ZETA JONES
HAS SHE? OR HASN'T SHE?

The Question The Whole Nation Is Asking When They Are Not Asking The Question About Billie

HAS she or hasn't she? It's the question the whole nation is asking when they are not *(I thought I had fired you. Ed.)*.

Has Welsh-born movie sensation Catherine Zeta Jones had her brain surgically removed? Here are the tell-tale signs:

1. **She has married the elderly Michael Douglas who is old enough to be her grandfather.**
2. **She has had her eyes done.**
3. **Er…**
4. **That's it.**

THE MAIL SAYS: WE AGREE WITH WHATEVER THE SUN SAYS

KIDS SAY THE FUNNIEST THINGS

So tell me again how he fell into the pool, mister...

A NEW so-called report claims that the children of working women get worse A-Level results than those of women who stay at home. Well, thanks a lot! As if us high-achieving career supermums haven't got enough on our plates, along comes this study (produced no doubt by *male academics*), which tries to unload another bucket of guilt in our in-trays.

Well, I'm sorry – I'm not going back to being the little woman at home, ironing Simon's underpants and cleaning up Charlie's sick. What do you think au-pairs are for?

And, for your information, Charlie is exceptionally well-balanced, has a reading age of 9½ (not bad for a four-year-old!) and his teachers are already asking us if we have put his name down for Oxbridge.

And that is entirely down to yours truly putting in the essential "quality time" or, as I call it, "Charlie time"!

Because although during the day I may be "Polly Filler, top columnist, writer and broadcaster", when I get through the door I'm just "Polly Filler, 100% mum".

And I'm fiercely protective about this. Nothing comes between me and my undiluted 40 minutes a day of "total C.T." (Charlie Time!).

It's a strict routine. As soon as I get home at 6.30pm we flop down together in front of "Cow and Chicken" on the Cartoon Network. At the end of it Charlie wakes me up and asks for a story. So, of course, I put on the story tape. (After all, the useless Simon is hardly going to apply himself to reading Harry Potter aloud when he's too busy watching "Hoover Wars" on E4 with Paul Ross and Angela Rippon.)

After ten minutes' solid literary skill development (and a much needed G&T for myself) it's off to Bedfordshire – or wherever else we've been invited to dinner.

Charlie goes straight to sleep and I can go out with a clean conscience. But, hey, don't get me wrong. I'm no saint! Like other busy mums with hectic schedules and high profile lifestyles, I sometimes have to juggle things around. Some nights (probably no more than a few times a week) even I can't avoid those "must-go" events: parties, launches, openings, gym sessions, girlie get-togethers and poker nights at the Groucho! So, I just have to put "Polly Filler, Mum" on hold while "Polly Filler, Breadwinner" earns the money for the luxuries in Charlie's life. Like staying in a fabulous Children's Hotel in Dorset while Simon and I go for a weekend's shopping in New York.

AND, another thing… if mothers didn't go out to work then think of the consequences. Our au-pair Irina would be at home in Slovenia looking after her kids instead of taking Charlie to McDonald's and allowing me to write this column. Think about it.

© Polly Filler.

"Yo, bitch… what's 'app'nin'?"

It Really Is Nepalling

A new short story from the pen of *Sylvie Krin*

(winner of the 1983 Betty Trash Award for Romantic Fiction)

THE STORY SO FAR: Charles and Camilla are watching Sky News as it reports the latest harrowing scenes in the tiny mountain kingdom of Nepal.

Now read on...

"IT REALLY is appalling." Charles gestured towards the 94in wide-screen Hirohito TV set, a gift from his friend the Emir of Dubya in return for a year's supply of organic chocolate chip and ginger oatcake from the famous Highgrove Biscuit Workshop.

"It really is appalling," he repeated to his beautiful paramour and life partner, as she poured them both a soothing nightcap of 140° Taliban whisky.

"I mean, Dippy was such a terrific chap when I knew him."

They both stared as the screen showed the burning pyre on which the old Etonian king-for-a-day was going up in wreaths of incense-laden smoke.

"I say, Chazza, what's going on? It's not more of that ghastly foot and mouth, is it?"

"No, old thing." Charles did his best to conceal his irritation at Camilla's lack of interest in world affairs and in what he called 'the you know, things that really matter'.

He explained to her that his old friend, the Crown Prince of Nepal, had unfortunately had a moment of madness and murdered his entire family with a Rach-maninov AK94 automatic sub-machine gun.

"I can't understand it," Charles murmured. "I remember once staying with him in one of his palaces at the foot of the Himalayas.

"I actually did a rather good watercolour from his veranda, looking out over what they call the Valley of the 17,000 Lotus Blossoms."

Charles took a sip of his nocturnal beverage as his thoughts turned to his beloved paintings. "It's the one on the landing upstairs, outside the room where I keep my polo things. You must have noticed it. Sir Hugh Casson said it was the best thing I ever did."

"Come off it, Chazza, the old toady said that about all of them," snorted Camilla topping up his tumbler with more of the exquisite amber fluid from the remote Highland distillery of Glen Iskinnock.

"I can almost smell those lotus blossom-thingies now," Charles mused, "the sun coming up over the distant peak of Mount Bunjijumpa, the sound of the monks chanting in the valley below..."

"I'm just popping out for a last fag in the garden," Camilla interrupted, a trifle brusquely, leaving Charles alone in a strange state of hypnotic reverie.

"I just can't believe it..."

"I JUST can't believe it!" barked the Duke of Edinburgh. Even at 80, his voice still carried the same unmistakable ring of command that had boomed out over the quarterdeck of the corvette HMS Intolerant of which he had been First Officer 60 years before.

"Don't be hard on the boy," said Her

Majesty the Queen. "It's not been easy for him having you as a father."

"Bollocks," harrumphed the Duke, as he gazed round at the room-full of his assembled relatives.

And what a shower the House of Windsor had become.

The Princess Royal, looking more like one of her damn horses every day.

The Duke of York, reminding him of the sort of fat boy he and his friends had enjoyed bullying at Gordonstoun.

That big girl's blouse, Edward, with his grasping wife.

And he didn't even recognise half of them. Who was the bearded Johnny who looked like the Czar?

And that other one who was always at Wimbledon kissing female tennis players? Damned if he could remember.

As for that woman in the wheelchair, was that really his sister-in-law? She

looked even older than the dear old Queen Mother who, frankly, was the only one he had any time for.

"I just can't believe it," the Duke reiterated. "After all these years, my damfool son has decided that he can't just go on keeping this woman of his as a bit on the side, as any sensible chap would do."

The Queen coughed irritably, kicking a corgi under the sofa to express her disapproval of her husband's nautical disregard of the estate of marriage.

"He's now insisting on a full-dress wedding in the Abbey, presided over by the Archbishop of Canterbury, the Chief Rabbi and some ayatollah-wallah with a beard and a tea towel on his head.

"Well, all I can say, is that Charles will marry her over my dead body."

His words were drowned by the deafening roar of a helicopter as it landed on the palace roof.

Within seconds, the French windows were shattered, as a uniformed figure in a balaclava and full battle fatigues leaped SAS-style into the room.

Rolling over expertly, he sprang to his feet brandishing a Terminator 3 assault weapon. It was Charles.

"Now listen to me, Pater and Co. I've had it right up to here with, you know, all of you.

"I'm jolly well going to marry Camilla, whatever you say. And you won't say anything, because you're all going to be deaded."

His voice broke into a manic Goon-style shriek.

With a final piercing cry of "Yin-tong-diddle-i-po," the Crown Prince of England prepared to squeeze the trigger and win his place in the history books by spraying the room with a deadly hail of lead.

"Really, Charles," his mother protested, "it's past your bedtime..."

"REALLY, CHARLES, it's past your bedtime." Charles woke with a start, to see his consort shaking his shoulder gently.

"Oh dear," he said, "I've just been having the most appalling nightmare. I didn't want it to end."

He rose shakily to his feet. What was it his old friend and mentor Sir Laurens Van der Post had so often told him about dreams, as they sat around the camp fire in the Kalaghasi Desert?

"Does the man dream of being a butterfly, or does the butterfly dream of being a man?"

How very true that was, whatever it meant...

© Sylvie Krin 2001.

SUPERMODELS

KERBER

POETRY CORNER

In Memoriam Desmond Wilcox, broadcaster

So. Farewell then
Desmond Wilcox.

You made TV
Documentaries
And appeared in them.

But you were best known
For being
Esther Rantzen's
Husband.

That's Life. That was her
Most famous programme.

Man Alive. That was
Yours.

It is what Keith
would call
Ironic.

E.J. Thribb (17½)

Lines on the 70th Birthday Party of Britain's Greatest Dramatist, Harold Pinter.

(Young man is seated at his desk in dreary south London bedsit. He writes and then reads aloud.)

So. Harold Pinter.
You are 70. *(He pauses)*

Curtain

E.J. Thribb (not yet 70)

"Brilliant!" MICHAEL BILLINGTON
"Unmissable" TIME OUT.

In Memoriam Larry Adler

So. Farewell then
Larry Adler.

Famous for your letters
To *Private Eye.*

Keith's Mum says
You also played
The mouth organ.

She says you met
George Gershwin, Cole Porter,
Duke Ellington, Louis Armstrong
and Charlie Chaplin *(That's enough names. Ed.)*

E.J.T.

NEW TORY LEADERSHIP CANDIDATE

The Belfast Telegraph

THE distressing scenes in British cities are enough to make one despair. Bradford, Oldham, Leeds, Burnley – the sectarian divides that have for so long festered in these communities have exploded into violence and hatred... cars set alight... youths throwing petrol bombs... police caught in the middle... every summer it's the same... water cannon needed... bloody British... cut the mainland loose and float it out to sea.

© *The Belfast Telegraph.*

"Trouble at t'Mosque..."

PRESIDENT BUSH ARRIVES IN MADRID

Ich bin ein Spaniard

OUTRAGE OVER BULGER RELEASE

Our Overkiller Staff **Phil Paper**

THERE was universal horror across Britain yesterday following the release into the tabloids of hundreds of articles about James Bulger's killers into the community.

"Despite the time that has passed since the terrible murder, these articles still seem almost childlike in the way the issues are laid out, revealing virtually no signs of maturity whatsoever," said one worried journalist. "Their arguments aren't near fully developed, and you can't hide the fact that people will search these salacious comment pieces out no matter how well hidden away in the features sections they are.

"Let's just hope the identity of the journalists responsible can be kept secret for the sake of their careers."

© *The Sun, The Official Big Bulger Paper*

I'm Full Of Hate, Anger And Shit

THE WORLD I live in is a world of hatred, anger and fear. Will I be sacked by the editor? Or will I be allowed to continue writing this rubbish every day?

My face tells the story – it is lined with grief, anguish and misery.

There is only one thing that keeps me going – the thought of the large cheques I earn by coming up with this drivel.

Anger. Hate. Shit. That is my world. Will I ever be able to lead a normal life again? Will I ever be able to smell a rose or see the sunset without writing 800 words on "Roses – don'tchahate'em?" and "Why can't sunsets leave us alone?" I do not ask for pity. I just want more money.

© *Lynda Lee Potty.*

BABY 'IS OWN FATHER'

by Our Medical Staff **Dr Frank N. Stein**

IN AN extraordinary scientific breakthrough, doctors in a Californian clinic have produced a baby by using its own foetal tissue to self-fertilise its reproductive cells in IVF conditions using the DNA from a GM soya bean. *(Is this right? Ed.)*

"It's amazing," said Dr Stein. "Baby X is his own father, brother, sister, mother, cousin and vegetable patch.

"This pioneering technique," he continued, "will benefit nobody at all but we have the technology and we have proved that it can be done."

Proud father Baby X was unavailable for comment last night as he is undergoing a sex change operation followed by surgery for breast implants and *(That's enough medicine. Ed.)*

ASCOT SHOCK

"And what do you do?"

"Cocaine, Ma'am"

"I'm in a public/private partnership with Mr Hyde"

NEW BBC SERIES

9.00 Monday BBC1

Chalk and Cheese

(concluding episode 9.00 Tuesday BBC1)

NEW original crime series with Inspector Chalk and Detective Sergeant Cheese. Dave Chalk is an old-style maverick copper who likes to break the rules, wherease Sally Cheese is a play-it-by-the-book fast-track graduate. Chalk is an alcoholic divorcé with a gay son and a complicated private life. Cheese is a working mother married to an inner city vicar and has to balance new baby with life in the elite NR7 squad. Can Chalk and Cheese resolve their differences and solve the Chinese triad drug-trafficking child abuse murder robbery case? Who cares? Starring Ricky Tomlinson as Inspector Chalk and Sarah Lancashire as DS Cheese.

Watch out for Ross Kemp playing Robson Green.

9.00 Wednesday BBC1

Fire and Ice

(concluding episode Thursday BBC1)

NEW original crime series starring Trevor Eve as Chief Inspector Derek Ice who teams up with senior pathologist Dr Hilary Fire (Samantha Bond) to solve the cases that are too boring for all the other police series to take on. Watch out for cameos by Ricky Tomlinson as Police Commissioner Robert Salt and his psychological profiler Dr Melissa Pepper, played by Sarah Lancashire.

Will they crack the mystery of how to fill in a couple of hours of midweek television without the public switching over? Watch out for Robson Jerome as Kemp Ross.

Eye rating: Z-z-z-z-z-z Cars was better.

Telegraph Fashion From Ascot

by Hilary Alexandra-Schulman

Lucy Nobby-Blonde in a silk dress by Fruti Kleevage and a Zilli hat.

Mrs Iama Mutton-Drestaz-Lamb in a Tuyung Foriu dress and a hat by Stoopede.

Mr Tristram Twerp sporting an embroidered waistcoat by Gitt with traditional topper from Snobbs & Crooks of Savile Row. (That's enough silly Asscot. Ed.)

ROYAL ASCOT

CHARLES AND CAMILLA TAKE THEIR PUBLIC RELATIONSHIP A STAGE FURTHER

"You're putting up too many walls..."

79

Letters to the Editor

The Decline In Modern Cricket

SIR – To those of us who have been out East and seen a thing or two, there is nothing new in the disgraceful scenes recently re-enacted on some of our leading cricket grounds as play was brought to an abrupt halt when the field was invaded by hordes of over-excited supporters from the Indian sub-continent.

I well remember a match in Hindujastan shortly before the last war, when the Viceroy's XI (Captain H. Gussett, 17th/21st Balti Volunteers) was playing a visiting team from the northern Punjab, the Fallalabad Ticket Collectors XI. Replying to the visitors' first innings total of 721 for 2 declared, we were making a spirited fight back on 12 for 6, when the Viceroy's ADC, Major Harry 'Toppo' Thompson, was bowled middle stump and gallantly refused to walk on the grounds that the delivery had been a no-ball. In this he was supported by the umpire, his junior officer Captain Bertram "Bertie" Berkmann.

It was at this juncture that over 30,000 enraged natives, high on the local *boxwalla* leaf (or bunji, as it is known), swarmed onto the pitch intent on reversing the umpire's decision.

Fortunately, disaster was averted by the prompt action of the watching Viceroy, Viscount Chadlington (later the Earl of Gummer), who ordered a batallion of the McDonald's Highlanders (the 'Whoppers') to open fire from a battery of quarter-pounders concealed behind the sightscreen.

Once the several thousand casualties had been cleared from the field, play was resumed, and we had no more trouble from pitch invasions, on this or any subsequent occasion.

Readers may incidentally be interested to know that Major Thompson went on to make 463 not out, taking the Viceroy's XI to a well deserved victory by 4 wickets.

H. GUSSET
The Old Pavilion, Arlott St John, Dorset.

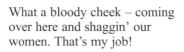

Another Taxi Driver Writes A Novel

This Week **Garry Bushell** (Cab No. 309472)

Chapter One
Blimey Guv! See the pair of jugs on that bird over there by the crossing? Wouldn't mind giving her one!

Chapter Two
Them asylum seekers?

What a bloody cheek – coming over here and shaggin' our women. That's my job!

Chapter Three
This country's gone to the dogs. All people think about is sex. Cor!! Look at the legs on that one pushing a pram. 'Er legs go right up to 'er whatsit.

Chapter Four
You ever written a novel, guv? Nothing to it. I've got my one 'ere. I'll sign it for you, if you like. No? You foreign or what?

Chapter Five
I 'ad that Dirty Desmond in the back of the cab. What a gent. He could do a lot of good for this country. Like give me a job.

Chapter Six
See this tattoo? If I move my arm, you can see that underneath the bird's tits it says "Vote UKIP". Clever innit? *(That's enough. Ed.)*

NEXT WEEK: Tony Parsons (Cab No. 757324).

10 TOP TIPS TO KEEP SUMMER HOLIDAY BOREDOM AT BAY

by Philippa Page

1 **Why not take your kids for a day-on-the-farm with a difference?**

With thousands of animals still being slaughtered by the men-from-the ministry, your kids can enjoy a "British-style safari", watching sheep and cows being blasted with shotguns by Defra marksmen. Seven days a week. And it's absolutely free!

Age Rating: 5-11

2 **If it's raining, why not let the kids loose on your computer?**

Your boys can use your credit card to download the latest hard-core pornography, while the girls can have fun on-line by joining internet chat rooms to meet real live paedophiles from all over the world.

Age Rating: 5-12

3 **Do your kids love McDonalds?**

Why not send them to work there? It's great value, at 3p an hour for a 16-hour shift. And it means you can stay home watching television, without them coming in saying "We're bored. What can we do?" *(You're fired. Ed.)*

Age Rating: 3-10

THE SUN SAYS

It's Great Beaten

● **Henman – you are a disgrace**. The whole country was behind you and you let us down. You scumbag. Is that the thanks we get for expecting you to win?

● **The British Lions – more like castrated mice. You are a disgrace.** The whole country was behind you and what did you do – LOSE!! You scumbags. Why don't you stay away for ever. Is that the thanks we get for cheering you on?

● **Nasser Hussain – you are a disgrace**. Even your brother Saddam would have shot himself this morning when he

heard the result. You loser scumbag. Is that the thanks we get for overlooking the fact that you are foreign and supporting you?

● **The Sun Newspaper – what a disgrace**. Those scumbags should all be *(Surely shome mishtake? Ed.)*

COMPLETELY USELESS MEN TO RECEIVE HUGE SUMS OF MONEY

by Our Corporate Affairs Staff **Phil Wallet**

A GROUP of entirely hopeless and totally incompetent men in suits are to be given very large bonuses for no particular reason.

The money is not performance-related nor is it in any way related to the success of their companies, which have been performing abysmally for several years.

BBC

A man with a plummy voice told shareholders: "These payments are in accordance with normal company practice, and they would receive them if they performed as badly in any other organisation."

Railtrack

A number of the men have in fact performed so badly that they have been asked to "restructure their careers outside the company".

They will receive even more money than the men in suits who are staying on, as a recognition of how totally useless they have been.

What They Will Get

Man With Beard, Director of Corporate Resources **Current salary**: £847,000. **Bonuses**: £2 million. **Additional benefits**: £3.5 million.

Man With Glasses and Big Desk, Head of Corporate Communications (Policy) **Current salary**: £1,047,000. **Bonuses**: £5.4 million. **Additional benefits** (including even bigger desk and corporate sauna in office): £7.6 million.

Woman on Thirteenth Floor, Co-ordinator of Corporate Strategy (Human Resources) **Current salary**: £314,000. **Bonuses**: £612,000. **Additional benefits**: None (due to her being a woman).

Fat Man With Red Braces, Director of Expensive Lunches and Lying to the Press **Current salary**: £2,412,000. **Bonuses**: £12,865,000. **Additional benefits**: Legover in office and use of corporate jet.

"Foreman of the jury, do you find the accused 'looks guilty' or 'not looks guilty'?"

I've thrown my fat into the ring

SAD FAREWELL TO THE MAESTRO OF THE DISPATCH BOX

THE HOUSE of Commons was packed to the rafters yesterday to witness the final onslaught by the greatest parliamentarian of this or any other age – William Hague.

MPs on both sides lamented the departure of the man responsible for some of the greatest put-downs in the history of the House of Commons.

His Finest Hours

To Mr Blair

"Are you having a bad blair day?"

To John Prescott

"Wake up, I'm asking you a question!"

On Lord Archer

"There is no question of Jeffrey's probity. He will make an excellent Lord Mayor."

On his own plans

"I am resigning. Goodbye."

To Mr Blair

"Congratulations on winning the election."

"Dad – who was William Hague?"

Letters to the Editor

SIR – If Mr Kenneth Clarke were ever to become leader of the Conservative Party, I for one would never vote Tory ever again.

GEORGE HEADBANGER
Kent

SIR – If Mr Iain Duncan Smith were ever to become leader of the Conservative Party, I for one would be forced to emigrate.

MONTY MIDDLEGROUND
Ex-Pat Club, Marbella, Spain

SIR – I have recently considered rejoining the Tory Party, only to find that they are considering electing as leader an unashamed Euro-phile who would do away with the pound and hand over our sovereignty to the faceless bureaucrats of Brussels. Not in a million years!

DOROTHY QUICKSAVE
Milton Keynes

SIR – I have recently considered rejoining the Tory Party only to find that they are considering electing as leader a raving, right-wing "little Englander" who would turn his back on Europe and bury his head in the sand. Not in a million years!

REV. K. STINKHORN
The Vicarage, Botley, Hants

SIR – Has the Tory Party taken leave of its senses? Just when at last it seemed it was about to choose a charismatic and dynamic leader who could have united the Party and taken us forward into a new millennium, he is cruelly tossed out on the final ballot. I refer of course to Sir Edward Heath.

B.B. BLASHFORD-SNELL
Clapham

SIR – As a lifelong Conservative, I am appalled by the spiteful language and offensive personal vilification which has characterised the recent leadership campaign. It is hard to know who has been the worst offender in this disgraceful war of words – the fat, idle slob Kenneth Clarke, with his beer-stained Barbour, the bald, nondescript toff Duncan Smith, or that foreign nancy-boy Portillo. When will we see the return of old-fashioned good manners?

DR VIJAY VERRUCA
Peebles

Honorary Degree for Yoko Ono

SALUTAMUS YOKUM ONUM CELEBRATISSIMA FEMINA ORIENTALIS ET QUONDAM UXOR JOHANNES LENNONE SUPERSTELLA MUSICALIUM ARTIUM ET MEMBRUM BEATLORUM SED FAMOSA IN OWNUS RIGHTUS QUAM ARTIFEX INSTALLATIONIS ET CONCEPTUALIS SED SUPRA OMNIA PUGNATRIX PER CAUSA PACIS UNIVERSALIS SUB SLOGANO "FACIEMUS AMOREM NON BELLUM" ET ADHERENS MACROBIOTICUM LENTILES ET LEGUMINES ET PSEUDA MAXIMA RIDICULOSISSIMA ET TEDIOSA ET GRASPINGENDA JAPONICA TOTALITER SINE TALENTE NUNC SALUTAMUS.

© Universitatis Liverpudliensis (quondam Polytechnicus Merseyensis) MMI.

THE HAS-BEANO

BORIS THE MENACE

The Numskull

I'VE GOT TO PROVE I'M FIT TO BE LEADER!

OH DEAR! AN ORIGINAL THOUGHT!
WE CAN'T HAVE THAT!
RIGHT WING VIEWS ONLY!
BRAIN DEPT
EYE DEPT
BLOCK EARS TO ANYTHING PRO-EUROPEAN
MOUTH PREPARE TO RECEIVE FOOT!
EAR DEPT

SO WHAT MAKES YOU THINK YOU'RE THE RIGHT MAN TO SUCCEED WILLIAM HAGUE?
TORY PARTY

I'M BALD AND UNELECTABLE!
PERFECT!

BORIS THE MENACE
GNASHER'S LEARNT SOME NEW TRICKS!

SIT!
KENSINGTON AND CHELSEA
HMM! NICE TORY SEAT!

BEG!
PLEASE LET ME BE LEADER!

ROLL OVER AND DIE!
R.I.P. GNASHER
VERY CONVINCING!

KEN BUNTER
DON'T LET ME CATCH YOU SUPPORTING THE EURO AGAIN!
BIKE SHEDS

PLATELL THE PERIL
HEE! HEE! MY SECRET DIARY'S GOING TO FINISH A CAREER!
VIDEO

MY OWN!
YOU'RE FIRED!
JK

What You Will Read

'Banged Up'

by Jeffrey Archer

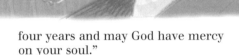

A new novel by the world's best-selling author.

Now read on...

"How do you find – guilty or not guilty?" The foreman of the jury stood solemnly as he faced the judge, "Guilty, Your Honour." Godfrey Bowman sat motionless, his world in ruins.

Yet he betrayed not one jot of what he felt. Beside him sat his faithful and fragrant wife, Margaret.

"Courage, Godfrey," she whispered. "You'll be alright. They won't send a great author like you to prison."

But it was not to be.

"Godfrey Bowman," declared the judge in solemn tones, "you have committed a grave and heinous crime. You are undoubtedly one of the most evil men who has ever stood before me in this court."

Bowman gasped inwardly. Yet still his steely blue eyes, which had put so many beautiful women under his spell, gave no hint of his inner turmoil.

"Regrettably," the judge continued, "in these so-called enlightened days it is not within my power to send you to the gallows. You will go to prison for four years and may God have mercy on your soul."

For a moment the packed courtroom reeled in shock. Then uproar broke out.

In the public gallery his former secretary the beautiful Adrina Farquharson-Dugdale collapsed in a swoon.

The shapely Annabella Lamont, for many years his most trusted confidante, threw herself to her death into the well of the court below.

"Silence!" cried the usher in a vain attempt to restore order to the court – that famous court where once Sir Oscar Wilde, Dr Crippen, and Lord Ha-Ha had heard their fate meted out just as he had.

Bowman stood erect. "Have you anything to say before you are taken down?"

"Excuse me," interjected the world's most distinguished writer. "I hear my mobile ringing. Hullo? This is Godfrey. I'm a bit tied up..."

He recognised the unmistakeable tones of his literary agent Victor Edward.

"Godfrey, we've just heard the verdict on BBC Five Live. It's perfect. There's a great book in it. 'Banged Up' – your life in prison. One of our people has already started writing it for you. You'll make millions! It's the best news we've had for a long time."

The End

VOICE OF The Moron

Conman who had them all fooled

HOW DID he ever get away with it? For years he held a position of authority, while at the same time lying and cheating to hold onto his job.

To many he was just a cheeky chappie, a loveable rogue with the gift of the gab.

But now the truth has been revealed. All along he was a share-dealing shyster who "filled his boots" and made up stories to cover his tracks.

One thing is certain. We will not be taken in by the likes of Piers Morgan ever again.

FRIENDS IN HIGH PLACES

THE TOAD I KNEW

by Our Man in Court **Kenneth Grahame**

ACQUAINTANCES of Mr Toad, who was sentenced to four years yesterday for the theft of a motor vehicle, were last night quick to distance themselves from the disgraced former grandee of Toad Hall.

Said Mr Ratty Rat of Riverside Villas: "I always knew he was a wrong 'un. Yes, we went to his parties and drank his champagne but we could tell all along that he would come to no good."

End of the Toad

Added another acquaintance, Mr Mole, "I turned a blind eye for many years to his obvious character defects. It was only going to be a matter of time before he ended up in prison."

Witty diarist and panel-game regular Mr Gyles Badger told the *Eye* "Whatever else you say about Mr. Toad, he was a hugely entertaining figure and larger than life character who added colour to the criminal world. He reminded many of us of that famous fictional character Lord Archer."

On other pages

SPOT THE DIFFERENCE

Jeffrey Archer

Bill Clinton

1. Manipulating cheat who indulged in a string of affairs

2. Lied under oath

3. Solicited grubby sex from a woman called Monica

4. In a cell doing bend and stretch for 'Big Ron'

1. Manipulating cheat who indulged in a string of affairs

2. Lied under oath

3. Solicited grubby sex from a woman called Monica

4. Hard-selling his memoirs on a lecture tour for big bucks

Kurdish Times

Jeffrey Archer Appeal

A terrible freak disaster has befallen Jeffrey Archer. Yet again his crop of lies has failed him and he now faces a bleak future without luxury penthouse flats by the Thames and Krug champagne.

But every individual, starving Kurd can make a difference.

Send whatever small cash you can spare to:

**The Jeffrey Archer Appeal
c/o A Tent
Northern Iraq**

All money donated will go directly to easing the plight of Jeffrey Archer with a small percentage kept to cover administrative costs (99.9%).

PLANE FLIES WITHOUT CRASHING

by Our Aviation Correspondent **Conor Curle**

THERE was amazement throughout the aviation world as a plane took off, flew around a bit, then landed again without turning into a fireball.

"It's incredible, I never thought I'd see anything like this in my lifetime," said a senior BA pilot. "The fact it could travel in the air means that the future of air travel is assured.

"Who knows, one day we may

see thousands of people every day travelling in the air without crashing."

CONCORDE STORIES RESUME

THE return this week of gushing PR pieces about Concorde into the newspapers has been declared an unqualified success.

"We thought these poorly written puff pieces had been mothballed forever after the plane blew up over Paris," said one delighted Editor, "but they quickly took off, and soon were travelling into the news pages at twice the speed of logic."

CAUGHT CIRCULAR

MRS LOLA ARCHER
The funeral took place yesterday at Cambridge Crematorium of Mrs Lola Archer.

A procession was formed as follows:

First Black Maria
Prisoner 74692 Archer J
Warder Ebenezer Screw
Inspector "Knacker of the Yard" Knacker

Second Car
Mrs Mary Archer
A Companion

Third Car
Sid Hack (representing the *Sun*)
Vince Snaps (representing the *News of the World*)
Mr Lunchtime O'Booze (*Private Eye*)
Mr Phil Space (*Private Eye*)

Fourth Car
Mr Georgian Snipcock
Mr Jeremy Tweed

Fifth Car
Empty
(Reserved for friends)

That's enough cars. Ed.

"Hallo there – I'm Roger from 'Claims Direct'..."

FOOT AND MOUTH STORIES 'DELIBERATELY SPREAD'

by Our Agricultural Staff **Paul Footandmouth**

THE Government has been deliberately spreading poisonous stories about farmers in the hope of diverting attention from its own incompetence.

The stories have appeared throughout the length and breadth of the media – all of them suggesting that farmers are overpaid millionaires who have deliberately infected their own animals in order to defraud the taxpayer.

A spokesman for the Prime Minister said: "This is completely untrue. I expect you have been talking to some greedy farmer who is trying to cash in on this disease."

RGJ

MORMON TUNNEL OF LOVE

IS THIS THE END FOR CHRIS EVANS'S CAREER?

by Our Showbiz Staff **Breakfasttime O'Booze**

THE MILLIONAIRE Chris Evans vowed last night that he would be back amid fears that his career as Britain's top drunk was over.

"I'll be back in the pub as soon as it opens," he told reporters. "Anyone who thinks I'm finished is wrong. I'm going to have another 17 pints."

Evans has established himself as the country's leading piss-artist with a record of drunken boorishness and alcohol-fuelled big-headedness second to none.

He shot to fame after his celebrated benders with fellow lout Paul Gascoigne and by last year he was worth £35 million a week to the breweries.

Yet last week he reached the highlight of his career when he downed 32 pints of Guinness, 14 bottles of champagne, 11 quarts of cider, 3 bottles of vodka and a litre and a half of Windolene.

But now Evans's glittering career as a tiresome inebriate may be cut short by his plans to go back to work.

But Evans was unrepentant last night. "I'm the best boozer in the business. No one can piss their life away better than me. You want a fight?"

Billie Piper is 18.

HOW KNACKER NAILED WORLD'S MOST EVIL MURDERER

by Our Crime Staff **Hugo Slavia**

THE BRINGING to trial of the world's most wanted mass-murderer Mr Slobodan Milosevic is a personal triumph for the British policeman, Inspector "Knacker of the Yard" Knacker, who has been on the trail of the man believed to be responsible for the death of 2 million Kosovans for over five years.

Said a tired but triumphant Knacker last night, "It was the toughest investigation of my life. We only had circumstantial evidence to go on, like articles we had read in the Daily Telegraph.

"But then came the breakthrough we had all been waiting for, when our forensic scientists identified a microscopic piece of dust which we had discovered in Mr Milosevic's trouser turn-up.

"When we examined this particle, only one millionth of a millimetre across, it at once became clear that it was identical to the type of dust found in many parts of Kosovo, and that the most hated man since Pontius Pilate would soon be swinging from the scaffold."

Watch Out, There's A Copper About!

THINKING of going for a walk down the street? Be careful what you take with you! A cigarette lighter, even an umbrella, could easily be mistaken for a high-calibre machine gun of the type which killed Jill Dando. In which case, the forces of law and order would be fully justified in gunning you down to keep the streets of our inner cities free for decent, law-abiding citizens to walk down unharmed.

ONE DEAD EVERY MINUTE

In today's fight against crime, speed is of the essence. That is why every year more and more people are run over by our highly-trained motorised division, as they race to the scene of another parking offence at speeds of up to 103mph.

Our advice is:

● leave your car at home
● avoid walking in the streets
● do not carry any suspicious-looking object, eg handbag, parcel, dog.

And, finally, do not stay in bed, as armed officers may well abseil through the window and shoot you through the head.

Issued by the combined police forces of the United Kingdom in the name of our new policy of zero tolerance, based on tolerating nobody.

REMEMBER
"It Could Be You"

GUILTY!

The Weirdo Obsessed With TV's Jill

by Our Crime Staff **Phil Paper**

NOW THAT the case is over, the true story can be told of a pathetic bitter loner who lived in a fantasy world and whose obsession with TV celebrities tipped him over the edge.

From his squalid room filled with old newspapers, clippings relating to the rich and famous and hundreds of photographs of women he has stalked, this dangerous lunatic ran the tabloid newspaper we now know as The Sun.

Said a psychological profiler, "Yelland fits the pattern perfectly. Of course we could have identified the wrong man. It could have been Paul Dacre or Piers *(cont. p. 94)*

I'm going to visit God now...

LORD LONGFORD
Tributes Pour In

By Our Obituary Staff **Bill Deads**

THOUSANDS of tributes flooded in last night as mourners queued to say their final farewells to the late Lord Longford known to millions as "that loony bloke who tried to let Myra Hindley out".

Diverse worlds met in their hour of grief to celebrate the life of the man they called "the bonkers peer who put porn on the map".

Those Tributes In Full

Myra Hindley "I'd be out by now if it wasn't for him."

Jonathan Aitken "He was a man of deep personal faith and a life-long believer in visiting the innocent."

Lord Archer "Lord Longford has come to see me every day. I was the last person to see him alive and he was convinced that I should be let out."

W.F. Deedes "I hope now that Private Eye's sheaseless shniggering at Frank will at lasht come to a full shtop."

WHAT YOU MISSED
Radio 4
The Today Programme

Sue MacGregor *(for it is she)*: Thank you, Jim, and now we've just a minute-and-a-half before the end of the programme to discuss the latest crisis in the Middle East. We've got Gideon Smitem from the Israeli Foreign Ministry and Dr Hamas Smitembak, speaking for the Palestinian Research and Stonethrowing Institute. Mr Smitem, if I could turn to you first, and I'd like to remind you that we've only got a minute left, could you sum up, as briefly as possible please, the entire history of Israel since 1948.

Smitem: Israel has to protect its security...

MacGregor: Well, that's your point of view, but I expect Dr Smitemback will want to say something rather different, and can I remind you that we've only got five seconds left.

Smitembak: We Palestinians have suffered...

MacGregor: Well, of course, not everyone would agree with you on that. But I'll have to stop you there because we've run out of time. So I'll just tell you a little bit about our next programme after the news, which is Desert Island Discs. And this week's Castaway is the former chairman of Railtrack, Mr Gerald Corbett.

Smitem *(still banging on in background)*: ...and then in 1967...

Smitembak: ...no, that is typical propaganda...

(Sound of scuffle)

MacGregor: ...and we've just heard news of a fight breaking out here in the studio. I can't see any dead bodies yet, but I'm hoping that I can soon talk live to myself about how I'm witnessing these terrible scenes taking place here in the Today studio...

(Fades into Desert Island Discs theme music)

Sue MacLawley: My castaway today is Gerald Kaufmann *(continued 94kHz)*

PUBLIC TO BE ISSUED WITH STUN GUNS

by Our Crime Staff **Rupert Murder**

IN A bid to halt the rising tide of police violence, members of the public are to be issued with a new high-voltage laser device.

The new stun guns will enable citizens to prevent the police from gunning them down in the streets or in their beds for no apparent reason.

The laser works by disabling an armed policeman at a range of 25.4 metres, without causing him any damage for which he could then claim millions of pounds in compensation from the taxpayer.

"I don't care if he does have Viking ancestry... We don't allow that sort of thing in the park"

Daily Mail

FRIDAY, AUGUST 10, 2001

Newspaper of the Year

HOUSE PRICES SLUMP TO HIGHEST LEVEL EVER

by Our Property Scare Staff **Abbie National** and **Hal E. Fax**

HOMEOWNERS face the terrifying prospect that by the end of the week their homes will be worthless, according to figures released by the Daily Mail.

Millions of mortgage payers could well be living in cardboard boxes by next Monday, if what the Daily Mail is predicting comes true.

Top property experts in the Daily Mail office were warning last night that a typical five-bedroom family house in North London, currently worth £750,000, will be worth only 20p by next Friday.

The typical owners of such a house could well see their daughters turning to prostitution

---
Rubbish
---

and their sons having to join gangs of Yardie drug-dealers in order to meet the mortgage repayments.

This terrifying but only too likely prospect is the direct result of the recent explosion in property values, fuelled by Gordon Brown's reckless public spending plans. *(Are you sure this is right? Ed.)*

Last month alone, house prices across southern England rose by a staggering 512 percent.

A one-room garden shed in Surbiton was sold for over £1 million within ten minutes of being placed on the market.

But all this means is that the crash, when it comes, as it surely will, will be infinitely worse than anything this country has seen since the last time there was a Labour government.

Perhaps the country will at last wake up to the realisation that Ken Clarke is the only man who can save us from repossession, negative equity, wholesale destitution and violent death at the hands of Triad money-lenders.

ON OTHER PAGES ● Does eating lamb give you BSE? 3 ● Does watching "Brass Eye" give you cancer? 5 ● Does reading the Daily Mail give you a bit of scare over your breakfast? 94

LADY ARCHER'S NEW THEORY ON SOLAR POWER

The sun shines out of Jeffrey's bottom

"You never play with me, all you ever do is read good parenting books"

THOSE BEIJING OLYMPICS

New Events

- **Shooting**: Student Target Event *(machine gun)*
- **Running Dog Races**
- **Putting The Shot** *(into the dissidents)*
- **High Jump** *(name of religion)*
- **Swimming** *(to Taiwan)*
- **Long March** *(4000 kilometres)*

V.S. NAIPAUL

WE regret that this feature cannot appear as Sir Vidia Naipaul walked out of the interview after the first question. When asked whether spoons loomed large in his Caribbean childhood he began to abuse the interviewer for not having read all his books. He then left the room. This popular feature will return next week when John Pilger will discuss the role of the spoon in American imperialism.

The Alarming Spread of IDS

BY OUR MEDICAL STAFF
DR THOMAS UTTERFRAUD

A LARGE number of senior Conservatives are believed to be suffering from the mystery illness known as IDS.

IDS affects both men and women and attacks the capacity to resist choosing the wrong leader. It produces softening of the brain and the eventual loss of all mental faculties.

Those who have already fallen prey to the IDS virus include Somerset Peer Lord Rees-Mogg, former Prime Minister Baroness Thatcher, former has-been Mr William Hague, the Editor of the Daily Telegraph Charles Moore, and top TV funnyman Mr Jim Davidson who (cont. p. 94)

Belfast Latest

PEACE TO BE DECOMMISSIONED

IN A major breakthrough, all parties in Northern Ireland have agreed to bury the peace process, and put it permanently "beyond use". Mr Gerry Adams last night accused Mr Trimble and the British Government of "betrayal" by using the peace process to destabilise the attempts to find peace. But Mr Trimble hit back by (cont. p. 94)

SPOT THE DIFFERENCE

MACEDONIA
British troops sent in to make sure the terrorists disarm

ULSTER
British troops pulled out even though terrorists refuse to disarm

 ### No. 94
Wee Donald The Miser

THERE ONCE lived in the town of Edinburgh a young man whose name was Donny Dewar. And he told the guid folk of Edinburgh that it was a sin to be rich. "Look at me," he would say. "I have given away all that I have, even my wife to the Lord Irvine of Lairg. And now I hae nothing at all, save only a crumpled suit, an iron bedstead and a wee bowl of porrage for my tea." And the guid folk of Auld Reekie so revered this worthy man that they raised him up to be the first citizen of the whole kingdom of Caledonia. "Donald is the best man amongst us," they cried, "for he abjures the baubles and bawbees of Mammon and wishes only to live a quiet and humble life, along with his bowl of porrage (see above)."

But then the day came when, sadly, puir wee Donald passed away. And when they came to look under his bedstead they found the following items, viz:

1. 450,000 shares in the Glaxo Drug and Armament Co.

2. 450,000 shares in South African Nuclear Tobacco.

3. An enormous pile of gold coins, £50 notes and Green Shield stamps to the value of three pounds, nine shillings and nine pence or one free toaster.

And the guid folk all threw up their bonnets in dismay and wrote letters to the Guardian saying that "Donny was nothing but an old humbug and we are all glad he's ganged awa' the noo."

Moral: Ye canna tak it wi' ye, ye ken!

"Does my drum look big in this?"

ROBERT THOMPSON

PORN WORLD SHOCKED BY BLAIR HOLIDAY REVELATION

by Our Pornography Staff **Rabbi Lionel Blue-Movie**

SENIOR figures from the world of pornography were shocked to discover that one of their top locations, The Chateau de Sade, was being used by Tony Blair and his family for "holiday purposes".

Said top male porn director Riccardo Desmondi, "This will give the place a bad name. What are my artists supposed to think when they engage in marathon steamy sex romps on the very table where the Blairs ate their breakfast? It will be a big turn-off, I can tell you."

Signor Desmondi continued, "I hire this place from a respectable High Court Judge. I had no idea that he had links with such people as politicians.

"I had intended to shoot my new blockbuster *Mr Whittam Smith Whips It Out* (PG) heres, but now I will have to think again and relocate to Ilford."

© *Reprinted from The Guardian.*

"Bored?! You can't be bored! I've dumped you with someone different every day this week!"

SUMMER HOLIDAY PLANNER

ROBERT THOMPSON

The DAILY DRIVEL

24 August 2001

CELEBS GO TO CINEMA

by Our News Staff **Philippa Front-Page**

A NUMBER of celebrities whom no one has heard of last night went to a film which wasn't very good. *(Reuters)*

OTHER TOP STORIES *(exclusive to all newspapers)*

● Old Woman Wears Bikini On Beach pp. 1-6 ● Young Woman Wears Bikini On Beach p. 8 ● Lots More People Whom You've Never Heard Of Wearing Not Very Much On Beaches pp. 9-36

MEDIA NEWS

■ Why Oh Why Is Our Circulation Plummeting? p. 10

An open letter to KATE WINSLET

said, for all of us who refused to kow-tow to the Fat Police. You're Absolutely Flabulous, I wrote in a celebration of your unashamed ampleness.

But now you have kicked your sisters in the teeth, given in to Hollywood land, slimmed down to a waif-like ten stone. What message is that, Kate, for ordinary women with children who can't afford fancy diets and fashionable therapies!

HOW many times do we have to say this? It doesn't matter what you look like – we can't all be a size eight like me. And we can't all hit the ideal weight of 8 stone (though I have!).

You're making women feel unhappy by flaunting your new movie star body all over the glossy magazines.

We loved you a lot more Kate when you were the size of an iceberg and my partner Simon said, "No wonder the Titanic sank with *her* on board," when we were watching the repeat on the SkyFoxGold Repeat Channel. Even my toddler Charlie preferred you when he charmingly remarked, "Mummy – why is that fat girl a famous film star when you are so much thinner and more beautiful that she is?" (Huh! Kids!)

So Kate Thinslet – stop being so obsessed with your weight. We're just *not interested*!!

Yours in sisterhood,

Polly Filler

Dear Kate

YOU should be ashamed of yourself! You've betrayed all of us working mothers who struggle to combine career and children without being slaves to male expectations about our appearance!

Honestly! How *dare* you lose weight after all the support we've given you over the years! When you ballooned up to 27 stone I wrote that it was no one's business but your own if you wanted to stuff in the cream cakes and look like the back of a bus. You were a role model, I

Film Highlights

Planet of the Yobs

HORROR film set in the near future where an astronaut arrives on Earth to find the planet taken over by ape-like creatures who have replaced human civilisation with their own primitive tribal alternative. Contains unsettling scenes of bad language, violence and football. Will the humans survive? Will the yobs wipe them out completely?

'A' LEVEL RECORD AS PASSES REACH 110%

by Our Education Staff
Michael Grade-Inflation

THE NUMBER of passes recorded in this year's 'A' Level results have increased for the 19th year running.

Said schools minister, Eslevel Morris, "We are thrilled that for the first time more people have passed 'A' levels than actually took them. This is a terrific tribute to the pupils, the teachers and most of all to this government.

"In Maths, for example," she continued, "87% got 'A*' grades, 42% got 'A' grades and 78% got 'B's or above."

Overall, girls did better than boys with the average sixth-form girl getting 17 'A' levels and 52 'AS' Levels. The average boy, on the other hand, managed only one pass grade in Cycling Proficiency and a fail in the 50 metres swimming badge.

A concerned employers' spokesman said, "There is a yawning gap opening up in this country between the figures that are released and what everybody knows to be the truth." (Surely 'boys and girls'? Ed.)

Eslevel Morris, however, denied that standards were slipping, "Anyone who says that is like, well, you know, just really so, I don't know, what's the word... durbrained. Yeah. Right."

The Eye Clearing Service

There are still places available at the following universities:

Bluewater University, Kent (formerly NCP Car Parks)
Nigella Studies (BA) 3-year modular course assessing the cultural significance and iconic status of Nigella Lawson in the 21st century.

Grades required: EFE

London Greenwich University (formerly the Millennium Dome)
Communication Technologies (BSc) 4-year degree course reading text messages on your mobile phone. Itz th 14u!☺

Grades required: EFF

The British University of Motoring (formerly The British School of Motoring)
Driving Studies (BSc) A six-week intensive degree course, including theoretical and practical modules with special study of: looking in the mirror, indicating and then pulling out.

Grades required: FFF

IMMIGRANTS TO BE TAUGHT ENGLISH

...and then we'll start on the rest of the country

DID THE HAMILTONS KILL JILL DANDO?
Police Investigate New Claim

by Our Crime Staff **Maddie Tupp**

POLICE are looking into fresh allegations linking Neil and Christine Hamilton with the murder of TV presenter Jill Dando.

Said Inspector Knacker of the Yard, "Someone in a pub said they thought the Hamiltons looked the type to assassinate someone so we are obviously giving the matter our fullest attention.

"Although the suspects have a cast-iron alibi due to their being in court at the time, I have put 300 detectives onto the case and will arrest the guilty couple in due course."

Complete Waste Of Police Time

Their names have also been connected with the Great Train Robbery and the Jack The Ripper case.

"We have recently had a report," Inspector Knacker concluded, "that Christine Hamilton is none other than Lord Lucan in disguise and her husband Neil may well be Shergar who (continued p. 94)

TV Highlights

Celebrity Sleepover
BBC1 Tuesday 8.00pm

An Essex household welcomes Neil and Christine Hamilton into their home for the night, only to discover later that their house guests had in fact spent the night having dinner with friends ninety miles away.

Eye rating: Someone's got egg on their face

FIRE, AMBULANCE OR MAX CLIFFORD?

999 EMERGENCY SERVICES

The Daily Mail ograph

Friday, 24 August, 2001

Charles To Marry Camilla – Official

by Our Royalty Staff Sally Season

THE QUEEN has given the go-ahead to the marriage of Prince Charles to his long-time mistress Camilla Parker-Bowles, we can exclusively reveal.

The couple are to wed, probably in a registry office, and almost certainly sometime in the future.

Pension Funds In Crisis

The decision is bound to spark a major constitutional row, which could well lead to a collapse in house prices. *(Surely 'the downfall of the monarch'? Ed.)*

This sensational change of heart by Her Majesty, the Daily Mailograph has learned, is the culmination of two years of careful planning by St James's Palace to win round public opinion to the idea of the heir to the throne marrying someone who is not Princess Diana.

This world exclusive has ben unearthed by a Daily Mailograph investigative reporting team from close analysis of an article in last week's Spectator magazine written by one of the most respected journalists in Britain, Peter Obore.

Says Obore, "According to this chap I met at a dinner party who knew someone who worked in the Palace, the Queen is definitely thinking of giving the green light to her son's marriage sooner or later.

"But don't quote me," the top royal source added, "because I am completely pissed."

Asylum Seekers Hit Million Mark

The report published in the Spectacularlyboring was confirmed by the magazine's highly-respected editor Mr Boris "Beano" Johnson in his influential "Another Voice" column in the Daily Mailograph.

"Cripes, it must be true," said Beano last night. "Obore never gets it wrong. He met this chap at a party apparently, and he gave a him the complete inside story.

"Take my word for it," said our star columnist, "this is one for the front page. It could bring down the government, or indeed house prices."

ON OTHER PAGES

Toenails Of The Famous – Can you match these close-ups of bare feet to the celebrities they belong to? 34-35

THE SUN SAYS

BIG BONKER!

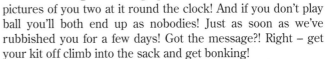

GO ON Paul – give Helen one for us!

Sun readers are crying out for you and Helen to have the Big-Brother-shag of the millennium. And we want to be there to take pictures of it. Yes, we do! And our readers deserve nothing less than graphic full frontal pictures of you two at it round the clock! And if you don't play ball you'll both end up as nobodies! Just as soon as we've rubbished you for a few days! Got the message?! Right – get your kit off climb into the sack and get bonking!

This is what we at the Sun are praying for. *(Surely "paying for"? Ed.)*

ON OTHER PAGES: Helen brushes her teeth **2** Paul goes to the toilet **3** Survivor's Charlotte does something not very interesting **4** Some other nobody does something else **5**

How dare people suggest I'm going round killing white people

I'm killing black people as well

"Hello? It's me, I'm on the toilet"

THE BOOK OF SHARON

Chapter 94

1. And lo again, it came to pass in the land of Is-rael that the Araf-ites and the Hamas-ites and all the other -ites waxed wroth, saying "Our land has been taken from us, and the children of Is-rael have pitched their tents even on the ground that has been ours through all generations."

2. Thou mayest have read this before, and thou knowest what comest next.

3. Then rose up a young man who was a Hamas-ite, and girded himself with the weapons of death.

4. And he went up into Jerusalem, unto the house that is called Pizza, where the children of the children of Is-rael were wont to gather.

5. And he slew them, even an hundredfold. And he was himself slain.

6. And there was much wailing and gnashing of teeth among the children of Is-rael at this terrible deed.

7. And they cried unto Sharon for vengeance.

8. And, lo, Sharon heard their cry and said unto them, "This is how we are repaid for trying to make peace with the Araf-ites."

9. "But now," saith Sharon to his people, "the time for talking hath passed."

10. And the children of Is-rael rejoiced with exceeding great joy. For they knew that soon the smiting was about to begin, as surely as the locust shall consume the harvest fields of He-bron.

11. And so the hosts of Sharon went forth into the lands of the Araf-ites and laid waste their dwelling places until not one stone stood upon another.

12. And the streets of those places ran red with the blood of the Araf-ites, even as the smiting continued until the setting of the sun.

13. And Sharon looked upon the smiting and saw that it was good.

14. "For," said he, "it teacheth them a lesson they will not forget in a hurry."

15. But thou dost not need to be an rocket-scientist to guess what happened next.

16. The following day another young son of Hamas girded himself with the weapons of death and went up unto Hai-fa, to repeat the whole sad story.

17. And there was much wailing and gnashing of teeth.

18. And the children of Is-rael cried out unto Sharon and sayeth, "What shall we do now, for this cannot be allowed to go on."

19. And Sharon said unto them, "I have a solution. From now on, it is no more the Guy that is called Mr Nice."

20. "Now I am really going to get smiting like I've never smote before."

21. And the children of Is-rael rejoiced. For this time, they thought, the smiting really will do the trick.

22. And thou dost not have to be an brain surgeon to know what cometh next.

(To be continued for ever)

The Gal looking for an asylum!

THEY'RE BACK!! The Ab Fab Gals!! Patsy and Edina, stoopid??!? They're bigger, better, and ballsier than ever before and don't they make us laugh??!? Hats off to BBC boss Greg Dyke for having the balls to bring them back!!? Crack open the Bolly sweetie darling and let's toast the funniest thing that's ever been on television!!?! Pop??!? Glug!! Glug!! Glug!! Absolutely fantastic!!!?!

OH NO!! Not them again!!?! Those two clapped-out caricatures who never made anyone laugh the first time!!?! That's Patsy and Edina for the lucky few who missed them!?!?

What's so funny about two batty old bags a-bingein' and a-whingein'!!?! All they do is get drunk and talk rubbish!!?! Who wants that??! *(You're fired.)*

Is that all you can think of, Mr Greg so-called Dyke??!? Well, pull your finger out and give us something original – like Only Fools and Horses!!?!

HATS OFF to plucky Posh for baring her soul to the nation and tellin' us all about her eating disorder!! Whatever you say, it took guts to come clean about looking like a skeleton in a mini skirt and boob tube!!?! Good on yer, Victoria!?!?

It'll help the hundreds of thousands of young girls across Britain who look to you as a role model and icon!!?!

Baroness Posh of Beckham!!! How about it, Mr Blair??!?

'OO DOES she think she is??! Posh Spice aka Victoria Beckham??! Gawd 'elp us, if we hadn't had enough of her already now she's written a book??! Tell you what, Posh, I read the first page and threw up!!! Talk about *thin* stuff – Geddit??!?!

Go on, clear off and take your daft hubby with you??!? *(No offence, David, the editor tells me we might be doing a promotional deal with your agent. G.S.)*

Byeeee!!

"It's not giving me the sense of freedom I anticipated"

Turn Your Lies Into ££££s!!

with the MAX CLIFFORD Creative Writing Course

"After a long day at work, Martin likes to come home, dump his work clothes and sprawl in front of the telly"

Britain's best-selling newspapers are constantly on the look-out for untrue stories about public figures.

Could you make up a story involving a famous person or persons and something to do with kinky sex?

My agency has an unparalleled track record in placing complete bollocks on every front page in the land – and you can make £75,000 or more.

IT'S 'MONEY FOR OLD RAPE' with MAX CLIFFORD

Mr M. Fuggee of Knightsbridge writes:
"He's fuggin' good, this fugger. Believe me, he's the fuggin' best in the fuggin' business."
Just ring, fax or email a 250-word synopsis of your cock-and-bull story and within days you could have the Essex police wasting huge amounts of police time and public money.

Coming soon

THE KING AND IDS

TOUCHING story of the bald, part-Japanese despot (Iain Duncan Smith) who falls in love with the bossy English nanny (Mrs Thatcher). Hit songs include:

"Getting to know you (because we hadn't heard of you till recently)"

"Shall we lose?"

"Hello, young Tories, wherever you are (we think your numbers are few)"

"Whistle a crappy tune"

"We kiss in the Shadow Cabinet"

(That's enough songs)

Cast In Full
Iain Duncan Smith **YUL BRYNNER**
Margaret Thatcher **PENELOPE KEITH**

I DON'T BELIEVE THIS... I DO NOT BELIEVE IT!!

OH WHAT DEAR... WHAT HAVE THEY PRINTED NOW?

NOTHING! ABSOLUTELY NOTHING! WE'RE NOT IN ANY OF THEM!

94

POSH SETS BAD EXAMPLE

by Our Celebrity Staff **Pierce Organ**

VICTORIA Beckham was yesterday accused of setting a bad example to middle-aged editors across the country by appearing with a lip-ring in public.

"Editors are very susceptible to this sort of thing," said a fashion expert. "And as soon as one of them inserts a pathetic non-story about Posh Spice into their paper they all start doing it."

Evidence that this was the case came from *Sun* editor David Hello, who said, "Of course I put in a lip-ring story. I put it right at the front of my paper. But so did all the other editors."

Ring of Truth

And when the lip-ring story later turned out to be "a fake" no one at the *Sun*, *Mirror*, *Mail*, *Telegraph* or *Guardian* was in any way embarrassed.

"So what?" said Alan Rubbisher. "As long as it gets us noticed then why shouldn't *(cont. p. 94)*

FOOTBALL TEAM WINS MATCH
Men Score Goals

YESTERDAY a football team won a match. One team scored five goals and the other team scored one.
(Reuters)

ON OTHER PAGES
● *England to win World Cup p. 2* ● *Britain to rule world p. 3* ● *India and Australia beg to rejoin Empire p. 4* ● *Should Michael Owen be the next king? p. 5* ● *Goals cheer cows as BSE is wiped out p. 6* ● *Beckham to run schools and hospitals p. 7* ● *Sven statue for Trafalgar Square plinth? p. 94*

Plus millions of pages of tributes and pictures

"Why didn't we think of that?"

NURSERY TIMES

Jumblies Refused Permission To Land

by Edward Fear

A BOATLOAD of green-headed, blue-handed asylum-seekers, known as "jumblies", were refused permission to land yesterday as fears grew that their craft, the SS Sieve, was "unseaworthy" and "unhygienic".

The origins of the jumblies are uncertain and an Australian spokesman would only say, "The lands where they live are far and few. The only thing we know about these people is their heads are green and their hands are blue. And we don't want their sort here."

The boat is now heading to the Hills of Chankly Bore, where they have been promised asylum.

ROY of ENGLAND

ENGLAND GIVE GERMANY A FIVE-ONE THRASHING...

THIS WILL REALLY SHOW THE WORLD WHO IS THE TOP FOOTBALLING NATION!

JA! SWEDEN

GOD SAVE OUR GRACIOUS SVEN!

J COOPER

TV Highlights

I Can't Believe We Watched That
BBC1 11.00 pm

A look back at hilariously bad television from the last few decades.

I Can't Believe We Watched I Can't Believe We Watched That
BBC1 11.30 pm

A look back at hilariously bad television from half an hour ago.

POISON CHALICE RESULT ANNOUNCED

"Congratulations! You lost!"

IDS NAMES HIS TEAM

by Our Political Staff **Hugh Cares**

THE NEW leader of the Conservative Party last night unveiled the team that is going to take the Tories into oblivion (Surely "power in the next election"?)

The new-look Shadow Cabinet that will rewrite the political map includes a mix of traditional heavy-hitters mixed with fresh new talent that will give the front bench a much-needed facelift.

OUT GOES
The bloke whose name you can't remember

IN COMES
A man who you've never heard of

OUT GOES
The fat bloke in the pin-striped suit

IN COMES
A pin-striped suit with a fat man in it. *(That's enough team. Ed.)*

'TORIANITY IS DEAD'
Admits Leader

by Our Religious Staff **Lucy Canon**

A SENIOR Conservative has admitted that Britain is "no longer a Conservative country".

"No one believes in it any more," he told worshippers (Sid and Doris Duncan Smith). "It used to be the backdrop to national life, but now it is just irrelevant. Faith in the basic tenets of Conservatism has dwindled away to nothing."

He further claimed that the Conservatives of England (CofE) faced a future as a small sect who no longer appealed to the mainstream.

Said one regular Conservative-goer, "We used to be a broad chuch, but now we are the Tory Party without a prayer."

WET TEE SHIRT COMPETITION

"Yes, this is the wettest"

EYE 2001 COMPETITION
SPOT THE ARSE

CLUE: *It's the one with the beard.*

That's enough 2001. Ed.